TODAY'S TIPS
FOR
Easy Living

Dian Thomas

HPBooks

Table Of Contents

Cover Photo: Dian's handy tips include (l. to r.) Fruit Totem Pole, Refreshing Fruit Pizza,
Sandwich Faces, Cranberry Ice.

Publishers: Bill and Helen Fisher; Executive Editor: Rick Bailey; Editor: Judith Schuler; Art Director: Don Burton; Book Design and Assembly: Tom Jakeway; Typography: Cindy Coatsworth, Michelle Claridge; Quality Editor: David Silverman

HPBooks
P.O. Box 5367   Tucson, AZ 85703   (602) 888-2150
ISBN:0-89586-167-4
Library of Congress Catalog Card Number: 82-80421
©1982 Fisher Publishing, Inc. Printed in U.S.A.

TV's Great Idea Lady

Nearly every TV-watcher in America recognizes Dian Thomas. She's a regular performer on the *Today Show* and has appeared on such major talk shows as *The Johnny Carson Show, Mike Douglas Show, John Davidson Show, Good Morning America, Phil Donahue, Canada AM, AM Los Angeles, Midday New York* and many others. Dian lost count after her 500th television appearance!

Millions of people have looked on eagerly as Dian taught Tom Brokaw, Jane Pauley, Bryant Gumbel and a host of other stars the fine points of cooking, camping, cleaning or just having fun. The huge bundle of mail Dian receives weekly testifies to the size of her TV following and the usefulness of her ideas.

But there's more to Dian than just television. She is the author of three very successful books. *Roughing It Easy,* her first national bestseller, catapulted her to fame. *Roughing It Easy 2* and *Backyard Roughing It Easy* cemented her reputation as an outdoor idea person. These three books are used around the world as rich sources for enjoying life outdoors.

There's theory behind Dian's clever, do-it-yourself approach. She holds a Master's Degree in Home Economics and has taught at Brigham Young University and a Utah junior high school. Each year Dian lectures and gives demonstrations to thousands of people who are anxious to hear her creative philosophy of living.

Dian's hectic schedule is filled with cross-country flights and rubbing elbows with TV stars. But she's still the genuine, down-to-earth person from Monticello, Utah, who found joy in improvising and making do. To Dian, every new day offers a chance to share a smile—and a great idea!

Where Do All These Ideas Come From?

Wherever I travel, people ask me the same question—where do I get all my ideas? My answer is simple. I grew up with a lot of them.

As a girl in southern Utah, I learned to make my own entertainment. My family lived in the mountains and we had to entertain ourselves. We often improvised games. One of my favorites was "Ingenuity." We'd take a commonplace object such as a cardboard box and see how many uses we could find for it. I was surprised at how many ideas we came up with.

In our home, we used our imaginations. There was always a sense of adventure in our family. We were full of curiosity and enjoyed each other's discoveries.

Today, I search for ideas everywhere I go. I'm always on the lookout for clever ways to do things. Just adding a bit of extra fun to an ordinary activity like a picnic or holiday can create a completely new experience. The more fun you have, the more you enjoy spending time with family and friends. With a little planning and effort, every activity can be more worthwhile and memorable.

My basic philosophy is simple: Make the most of each moment. Look for fun, innovative ways to enjoy every activity. Try a new approach to an old task. Spend time—not money—to make life more interesting.

The ideas for this book come from many different people and places. The aim is to provide you with material for hours of creativity and fun in your home. If this book helps your family work together, be creative and have fun, then my goal has been accomplished.

Today, I still play "Ingenuity." But now it's before an audience of millions of television viewers. Most ideas in this book have been done on TV. I hope you'll have as much fun using them as I've had creating and collecting them.

Dian shows Jane Pauley how to make a Tomato-Soup Cake.

Food Fun

Food is a very important part of family life. Mealtime is one of the few regular times families gather together. Holidays are special because they involve creating and sharing treats and feasts.

This chapter will give you delicious and inexpensive ideas. Use them to create nutritious meals and snacks for your family. Have fun making new food dishes and treats. Enjoy the time your family spends together discovering the wonderful world of food.

I've tried to give you some inspiration for every meal of the day. Breakfast is vitally important to every member of the family. Brighten your mornings and give your family a nutritious start with my Handy Breakfasts.

More people are bagging their lunch. The section on Brown-Bag Lunches has many pointers to pep up treats from home.

I've included Quick-Prep recipes to save time while you give your family the well-balanced meals they need. The Food Hints section gives you hard-to-find homemade recipes, emergency substitutions and some tips to rescue meals from the brink of disaster.

HANDY BREAKFASTS

Get up and get going! Begin with a nutritious, delicious treat and you'll start your day off right. Whether you're a faithful breakfast eater or one who has trouble finding time for a morning meal, you'll want to try these super breakfast foods. They're fast, easy to prepare and nutritious.

ADD GO-GO TO SO-SO BREAKFASTS

Add interesting, unusual ingredients to regular foods. They make breakfast too tempting to miss. Pep up your morning by adding these new or different foods to traditional breakfasts.

Sausage Stack—Top toasted English-muffin halves with cooked sausage patties, pineapple slices and shredded cheese. Broil until cheese melts.

Quick Scones—Cut English-muffin halves in quarters and dip in pancake batter. Fry in 1/4 inch of oil for scones. Serve with whipped honey and margarine or butter spread, powdered sugar or syrup.

Muffin-Tin Breakfast—Bake breakfast in non-stick muffin tins. To prepare breakfast for three to six people, preheat oven to 375F (109C). Line 6 muffin cups with a round slice of ham about the size and thickness of a bologna slice. Break egg onto each piece of ham. Salt and pepper egg. Line six more muffin cups with paper liners. Fill each 2/3 full with muffin batter. Bake 15 to 20 minutes or until eggs are desired firmness and muffins are golden brown.

French-Toast Sandwich—Make French toast and freeze. In the morning, put two pieces in the toaster. When they pop up, place cheese and ham slices between them. Wrap with paper napkin. Napkin comes in handy for wiping fingers.

Pancakes Plus—Add berries, sliced peaches, pineapple, chopped apples, nuts, raisins and bits of ham to pancake batter for extra nutrition and great taste. Or pour pancake batter on grill and sprinkle extras on top. You can prepare several varieties of pancakes using the same batter.

Waffle-Iron Breakfast—Place several strips of bacon on a waffle iron. Cook until done and remove bacon. Remove excess grease with a folded paper towel. Dip bread slices in mixture of 2 beaten eggs mixed with 2 tablespoons milk. Bake as waffles. Serve with bacon slices on the side. If your family eats in shifts, use half the waffle iron for bacon and half for French toast.

COMMUTERS' BREAKFASTS

Before you rush off, try something tasty and full of nutrients. These combinations will help you save time and eat nutritiously.
- Slice of cheese on whole-wheat bread.
- Yogurt and bagel.
- Crackers, cheese and carrot sticks.
- Slice of salami or liverwurst, French roll and milk.
- Slices of celery filled with peanut butter or cheese spread.
- Scrambled eggs wrapped in a flour tortilla, like a burrito. Add a teaspoon of chopped green chili for extra flavor.
- Scrambled eggs mixed with chopped chives and dash of sour cream or plain yogurt, served in pita bread.
- A mug of cream-of-tomato soup and whole-wheat toast.
- One-half cantaloupe filled with granola and milk.

30-SECOND BLENDER BREAKFASTS

Plug in your blender for some tasty, wake-me-up combinations. Blend all ingredients together. Serve immediately. Each makes 1 to 2 servings.
- 1 banana, 1/4 cup pineapple (chunks, slices or crushed), 1 cup milk, 2 tablespoons orange-juice concentrate, 1 egg.
- 1 cup cranberry juice, 2 tablespoons orange-juice concentrate, 1 egg, 1 cup milk.
- 1 cup peaches (with or without syrup), 1 cup milk, 2 tablespoons wheat germ, dash nutmeg or cinnamon.
- 2 tablespoons orange-juice concentrate, 1 banana, 2 tablespoons smooth peanut butter, 1 cup milk, 1 egg.

BROWN-BAG LUNCHES

More people are bagging their lunch. It's economical and more enjoyable than fighting lunch lines. Bring wonderful creations from home and make eating lunch an experience, not just a way to pass time. Be creative! Transform conventional lunches into delicious, fun-to-eat treats. It's easy if you try some of these tips.

SANDWICH ALTERNATIVES

Lunch tastes better when you eat unexpected treats. Add zest to your lunch by packing some alternatives to sandwiches.

Fresh Dip—Take along a plastic container of your favorite dip and fresh vegetables such as raw cauliflower, broccoli, carrots or celery. Boiled eggs and chips are also good. Combine your favorite powdered salad-dressing mix with plain yogurt for a delicious, low-calorie dip.

Inside-Out Sandwich—Roll a slice of luncheon meat and a slice of cheese around a bread stick. Stick toothpicks through top to hold.

Walking Salad—Slice off top of an apple. Hollow out core, leaving bottom of apple intact. Brush hollow with lemon or pineapple juice. Fill with peanut butter mixed with raisins, cream cheese or caramels. Replace top of apple and pack in plastic wrap or sandwich bag.

Peanut-Butter Switch—When you make your next peanut butter sandwich, exchange graham crackers for bread. Children will love this tasty surprise.

PEPPING UP SANDWICHES

Add unusual ingredients to conventional sandwich fillings or make your own fillings from scratch. Try the following super sandwich ideas.

- Add raisins, coconut, crushed pineapple or honey to peanut butter.
- Chopped nuts, celery, green pepper, pickle relish, olives, sunflower seeds or onions perk up tuna filling.
- Mashed avocado, with a drop of lemon juice, crisp bacon pieces and chopped onion makes a tasty filling.
- Mix mashed banana, peanut butter and a little frozen orange-juice concentrate together.
- Cream cheese mixed with chopped celery, nuts and raisins creates an appealing sandwich.

LESS MESS, FRESHER FOOD

- Cake can be messy because of crumbs. To avoid crumbs, bake cupcakes in flat-bottom ice-cream cones. Cones add crunch, too.
- For iced sheet cake or frosted brownies, cut a piece in half. Invert so icing is in the middle, sandwich-style. Wrap in plastic wrap. Eat without getting icing all over.
- To keep moist sandwich filling from making bread soggy, spread bread to the edges with butter or margarine before adding sandwich filling.
- Lettuce will stay crisp if you pack it in a separate plastic bag. Add lettuce to sandwich when you're ready to eat. Wrap a damp paper towel around lettuce, celery or carrot sticks before placing in plastic wrap or plastic sandwich bags. Moisture keeps vegetables crisp and fresh. Paper towel can be used as a hand wipe at lunch.
- Keep sandwiches, fresh vegetables, salads or other foods cool by using a fruit-juice cooler. The night before, pour juice into container with airtight lid leaving about 1 inch for expansion. Plastic tumblers with snap-on lids work well. Some juices can be frozen in individual portion-size cans.

Put juice in freezer overnight. Pack frozen juice container with lunch. It's a good idea to place juice container in a plastic bag to catch moisture that collects as juice defrosts.

When you're ready to eat, juice should be icy and ready to drink or eat as slush. Food will be cool and fresh as well.

DOLLAR-WISE TRICKS

Buy Ham On Sale—Ask the butcher to slice it very thin. Freeze individual sandwich-size portions in plastic bags. When you want a ham sandwich for lunch, pack frozen sliced ham along with bread prepared for a sandwich. It will be thawed and ready to eat by lunchtime.

Make Your Own Pita Bread—Use the accompanying recipe to make your own delicious pita bread. Fill bread with your favorite filling. Try chicken, tuna salad or peanut butter and honey.

Pita Bread

A wonderful way to create new sandwich treats.

1 envelope active dry yeast (1 tablespoon)
1-1/4 cups warm water (105F, 40C)
3-1/4 to 3-3/4 cups all-purpose flour
1/4 cup shortening
1-1/2 teaspoons salt

In a large bowl, soften yeast in warm water. Add 2 cups flour, shortening and salt. Beat with electric mixer on low speed for 30 seconds. Scrape side of bowl. Beat 3 minutes at high speed. With a spoon, stir in enough of remaining flour to make a stiff dough. Turn onto a lightly floured board and knead 3 to 5 minutes or until dough is smooth, elastic and slightly soft. Cover dough and set in warm place for 15 minutes. Divide into 12 equal portions. Flour your hands. Roll each piece between your hands to form a smooth ball. Cover with damp cloth and let rest 10 minutes. Gently flatten balls without creasing dough.

Banana Dog—Spread peanut butter and honey on a hot dog bun. Wrap in plastic and place in lunch with banana. At lunchtime, peel banana and place in hot dog bun for an unusual treat.

Peanut Butter And Honey Mix—When your peanut butter jar is half empty, add homogenized honey to taste and mix. It'll save time and mess when you want to make a quick peanut-butter-and-honey sandwich. Use within one month.

Cover and let rest another 10 minutes. Keep covered until ready to use.

On well-floured surface, lightly roll 2 pieces of dough into 2 7-inch circles, turning dough over once. Use enough flour so dough does not stick, stretch, tear or crease. Roll only from the center to outside edge. If you roll back and forth, dough will not puff as evenly. Arrange 2 dough circles on a baking sheet.

Preheat oven to 450F (230C). Bake for 3 minutes on ungreased baking sheet. Turn and bake additional 3 minutes. Bread should be puffy and golden brown. Bake each batch before rolling out the next. Carefully slice pockets in one end of each cooled bread using a sharp knife. Wrap while bread is warm. Store in plastic bag. Pita bread is softer and not as fragile on second or third day after baking. Makes 12 pita-bread rounds.

d? Do you hate to cook?
ods will appeal to you.
gelling, but they need
ion time. All of them

Salads

Miracle Green Salad

This salad keeps several days.

1 small head lettuce
1 cup celery, diced
1/2 cup green onions, diced
1 (10-oz.) pkg. frozen peas, thawed
1 (6-oz.) can sliced water chestnuts, drained
1/2 cup mayonnaise
1-1/2 cups dairy sour cream
1/2 cup grated Parmesan cheese
1/4 cup crumbled, cooked bacon

Break lettuce into pieces. Line bottom of a round serving dish. Layer celery, green onions, peas and water chestnuts. In a small bowl, mix mayonnaise and sour cream. Spread over vegetables. Sprinkle Parmesan cheese and bacon on top. Cover with plastic wrap and refrigerate overnight. Serves 6 to 8.

Mandarin Salad

A tangy gelatin salad!

1 (3-oz.) pkg. orange gelatin
1 (12-oz.) container whipped topping
1 (10-1/2-oz.) can mandarin oranges, drained
1 (15-oz.) can crushed pineapple, drained
1 (6-oz.) can frozen orange-juice concentrate, thawed

In medium bowl stir gelatin and whipped topping until smooth. Add oranges, pineapple and orange juice. Refrigerate until set. Any fruit combination works well. Serves 8.

Main Dishes

Lemon-Fried Chicken

Delicious, easy-to-prepare chicken.

1/2 cup all-purpose flour
Salt and pepper to taste
4 whole chicken breasts, skinned, boned,
   cut in 1-inch cubes
1/3 cup butter or margarine
2/3 cup lemon juice
2 cups hot cooked rice

Combine flour, salt and pepper in a pie plate. Roll chicken cubes in flour mixture until coated. Melt butter or margarine in large skillet. Add coated chicken cubes. Stir constantly over medium-high heat until browned, about 3 to 5 minutes. Sprinkle lemon juice evenly over chicken. Stir until steam from lemon juice evaporates. Serve immediately with cooked rice. Serves 4.

Rice Pizza

A different pizza treat!

2 cups cooked rice
1/4 teaspoon salt
1 egg
2 cups finely shredded Mozzarella cheese (8 oz.)
1 (16-oz.) jar pizza sauce
Favorite pizza ingredients

Preheat oven to 350F (175C). In a large bowl, combine rice, salt, egg and 1 cup cheese. Press over bottom of 12-inch pizza pan, making outer edge slightly higher. Top with pizza sauce and favorite pizza ingredients. Bake 25 minutes. Sprinkle with remaining cheese. Bake 5 minutes until cheese melts. Makes one 12-inch pizza.

Chili/Chip Casserole

A quick and easy supper.

1 lb. hamburger
1 (8-oz.) can tomato sauce
1 (16-oz.) can chili con carne
3 cups corn chips
1 small jalapeño pepper, chopped
1/2 cup grated Cheddar cheese

Brown hamburger in a skillet over medium heat. Drain off drippings. Add tomato sauce and chili con carne. Stir in 1 cup of corn chips. Heat until warm. Add chopped jalapeño pepper and grated cheese for added zip. Top with remaining corn chips. Serves 4 to 6.

Lemon-Fried Chicken.

Ham Broil

...ese and chicken combination.

...breast fillets,
...oned
2 slices ham, 1/4-inch thick
2 slices Swiss cheese, 1/8-inch thick
1 tomato, sliced, or 2 cups mixed salad

Broil chicken breasts until cooked thoroughly. Top each cooked chicken breast with a slice of ham and a slice of cheese. Broil until ham is hot and cheese is melted. Serve with sliced tomatoes or salad. Serves 2.

Desserts

Fruit Pistachio Dessert

A tasty pistachio delight.

1 (16-oz.) container whipped topping
1 cup miniature marshmallows
1 (6-oz.) pkg. instant pistachio pudding mix
1 (16-oz.) can crushed pineapple
1/2 cup chopped nuts

In large bowl stir whipped topping until smooth. Add marshmallows and pudding mix. Stir in pineapple with juice and nuts. Refrigerate at least 1 hour. Serves 5 to 6.

Tomato-Soup Cake

Unbelievable!

1/2 cup shortening
1-1/3 cups sugar
2 eggs
2 cups all-purpose flour
1 tablespoon baking powder
1 teaspoon baking soda
2 teaspoons allspice
1 teaspoon cinnamon
1 (10-3/4-oz.) can condensed tomato soup
1/4 cup water
1 cup walnuts, chopped
1/2 cup raisins

Preheat oven to 350F (175C). Grease and flour 9x13" pan or Bundt pan. In medium bowl, cream shortening and sugar. Add eggs and beat until fluffy. Sift dry ingredients. Mix tomato soup and water. Add sifted ingredients and soup mixture alternately to creamed mixture. Fold in nuts and raisins. Pour into pan. Bake 30 minutes in 9x13" pan or 40 minutes in Bundt pan. To frost, blend 2 tablespoons butter or margarine, 3 ounces cream cheese, 2 cups powdered sugar and 2 teaspoons vanilla until smooth. Spread over warm cake.

Quick Cupcake-Cones

Use your microwave to bake treats.

1 egg carton
12 to 18 flat-bottom ice-cream cones
1 (18-oz.) pkg. cake mix
2 eggs
1 (21-oz.) can pie-filling

Cut bottoms off egg carton. Insert cones in holes so egg carton holds them upright. Mix cake mix, eggs and pie filling. Fill cones 2/3 with batter. Bake in microwave 30 to 40 seconds on full power for 1 cone; 15 seconds longer for 2 cones. Let cones stand in oven 2 minutes after cooking is completed. Makes 12 to 18 cones.

Rich Chocolate Frosting

Tastes heavenly.

1 pt. whipping cream
1 (14.3-oz.) pkg. chocolate frosting mix

Whip cream in medium bowl until thick peaks form. Fold in frosting mix. Refrigerate 3 to 4 hours. Makes deliciously light chocolate frosting. Frosts one 9-inch, 2-layer cake.

Banana-Sour Cream Pie

Better than banana-cream pie.

1 (6-oz.) pkg. instant vanilla-pudding mix
2 cups milk
1/2 cup dairy sour cream
1 (9-inch) baked pie shell
2 to 3 bananas, sliced
Whipped cream or whipped topping, if desired

Prepare pudding with milk according to package directions. Stir sour cream until smooth. Fold sour cream into pudding. In pie shell, layer 1/3 of pudding and 1/3 of bananas. Repeat layers two more times. If desired, top with whipped cream or whipped topping or banana slices dipped in pineapple or lemon juice to prevent darkening. Refrigerate 1 hour or until ready to serve. Makes one 9-inch pie.

Sherbet Ice Cream

Super-smooth sherbet.

1/2 gallon softened sherbet
1 (8-oz.) container whipped topping

Fold ingredients together in a large bowl. Leave in bowl or spoon into containers. Place in freezer until firm. Serves 8 to 10.

Creamy Coconut Pie

Fast and easy, great-tasting pie.

1 (3-oz.) pkg. cream cheese, softened
1 tablespoon sugar
1/2 cup milk
1/2 teaspoon almond extract
1-2/3 cups flaked coconut
1 (8-oz.) container whipped topping
1 (9-inch) graham-cracker crust

Combine cream cheese, sugar, milk and almond extract in blender. Cover and blend at low speed for 30 seconds. Pour into large bowl. Add 1-1/3 cups coconut. Fold in whipped topping. Pour into crust. Refrigerate overnight. Preheat oven to 350F (175C). If desired, toast 1/3 cup coconut by placing it in a pie pan in the oven for 5 minutes. Watch carefully; coconut burns easily. Stir once during toasting. Garnish chilled pie with toasted coconut, if desired. Makes one 9-inch pie.

No-Fuss Banana Cake

No dishes and only one fork to clean!

2 ripe bananas
2 eggs, slightly beaten
1/3 cup vegetable oil
1 tablespoon vinegar
1 teaspoon vanilla extract
1 teaspoon baking soda
1 (18-1/2-oz.) pkg. banana cake mix
1 cup chopped nuts
Lemon Frosting, see below

Lemon Frosting:
1/3 cup butter or margarine, softened
1 tablespoon lemon juice
1-1/2 cups confectioner's sugar

Preheat oven to 350F (175C). In a Bundt or angel food cake pan, mash bananas with fork. Add eggs, oil, vinegar and vanilla. Beat with fork. Stir in baking soda. Stir in cake mix and nuts. Bake about 35 minutes or until toothpick inserted in center comes out clean. Cool on rack 10 to 15 minutes. While still warm, frost with Lemon Frosting. Serves 8 to 10.

Lemon Frosting:
Combine all ingredients in a medium bowl. Makes about 2/3 cup.

Instant Pie Crust

Made in one pan.

1-1/2 cups all-purpose flour
1-1/2 teaspoons sugar
1/2 teaspoon salt
1/3 cup, plus 1 tablespoon, oil
2 tablespoons milk or lemon juice

Preheat oven to 400F (205C). Mix flour, sugar and salt in 9-inch pie pan. In measuring cup, stir together oil and milk or lemon juice. Pour into flour mixture. Stir with fork until liquid is absorbed by flour mixture. Use fingers to press dough over bottom and up side of pan. Flute crust edge. Prick bottom with fork. Bake 12 to 15 minutes or until golden brown. Makes one pie crust.

Heavenly Chocolate Pie

So rich and so easy.

1 (1/2-lb.) chocolate bar with almonds
1 (12-oz.) container whipped topping, thawed
1 (9-inch) chocolate-cookie pie crust

Shred about 2 tablespoons from chocolate bar onto square of waxed paper with a potato peeler. Place in refrigerator until ready to garnish pie. Melt remaining chocolate bar in top of double boiler. Cool slightly. Gradually fold in whipped topping. Pour into chocolate-cookie pie crust, mounding slightly higher in center. Sprinkle top with chocolate shreds. Makes one 9-inch pie.

Graham-Cracker Bars.

Graham-Cracker Bars

A delicious graham-cracker treat.

1/2 cup butter or margarine
1-1/2 cups graham-cracker crumbs
1 (14-oz.) can sweetened condensed milk
1 (6-oz.) pkg. chocolate pieces
1-1/3 cups flaked coconut
1 cup chopped nuts

Preheat oven to 350F (175C). In oven, melt butter or margarine in a 9x13" pan. Sprinkle graham-cracker crumbs over margarine. Pour condensed milk evenly over crumbs. Top evenly with chocolate pieces, coconut and nuts. Press down gently. Bake 25 minutes or until lightly browned. Cool thoroughly before cutting. Store at room temperature. Makes 24 bars.

Saltine-Cracker Pie

Crackers never tasted so good.

3 egg whites
1 cup sugar
12 individual saltine crackers, crumbled
1 cup chopped walnuts
1 teaspoon vanilla
1 teaspoon baking powder
1/2 pt. whipping cream
1/2 teaspoon vanilla
3 tablespoons powdered sugar

Preheat oven to 350F (175C). Grease pie pan and set aside. Beat 3 egg whites until stiff. Gradually stir in 1 cup sugar. Add crackers, chopped walnuts, 1 teaspoon vanilla and baking powder. Mix thoroughly. Put in pie pan. Bake 30 minutes. Cool. Beat whipping cream, 1/2 teaspoon vanilla and powdered sugar. Spread on pie. Refrigerate 3 to 4 hours. Makes 1 pie.

Candy-Apple Parfait

A different apple dessert.

10 to 12 apples
1 cup water
1/2 cup cinnamon candies
1 (8-oz.) container whipped topping

Peel, core and slice apples into saucepan. Add water. Cook apples until tender. Add cinnamon candies and stir until melted. For a fancy parfait, layer apple mixture with whipped topping in serving dishes. Serves 6 to 8.

HANDY HINTS FOR COOKS

Did you ever want to make something and didn't have the recipe? Ever have a recipe that called for an ingredient you didn't have? Ever scorch the stew, try to eat soggy crackers or wonder what to do with leftover bread?

This section tells you how to solve these and scores of other cooking problems. It's packed with tips and hints I've collected. One is sure to be a disaster-saver for you!

HARD-TO-FIND HOMEMADE RECIPES

These clever little recipes often save the day. Keep them handy to use when they're really needed.

Sweetened Condensed Milk

You can't beat the price!

1 cup water
2 cups sugar
1/4 cup butter or margarine
4 cups instant milk powder

Combine water and sugar in medium saucepan. Stir over medium heat until sugar dissolves. Pour mixture in blender. Add butter or margarine. Blend on low, gradually adding milk powder. Blend on medium until smooth. Makes about 3-1/2 cups, enough to replace 2 (14-oz.) cans sweetened condensed milk.

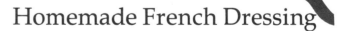

Homemade French Dressing

Tastes great on any salad.

1 (10-1/2-oz.) can condensed tomato soup
1/2 cup vegetable oil
1 teaspoon dry mustard
1 teaspoon salt
3 tablespoons sugar
1 teaspoon paprika
1/2 cup white vinegar
1 teaspoon onion juice or small white onion, minced

Combine all ingredients in a small bowl. Blend with electric mixer or blender until thickened. Pour into jar with tight-fitting lid. Store in refrigerator. Makes 1-1/2 cups.

Easy French Dressing

This dressing is easy to make.

1 (10-1/2-oz.) can condensed tomato soup
1/3 cup sugar
1/3 cup vinegar
1/3 cup vegetable oil

Combine all ingredients in bottle or jar with tight-fitting lid. Shake well. Shake again each time before using. Store in the refrigerator. Makes two cups.

White Sauce Cubes

An easy way to save time.

2 cups butter or margarine
2 cups all-purpose flour
1/4 cup chopped chives
1/2 teaspoon poultry seasoning
1/4 teaspoon crushed dried sage
2 tablespoons dried minced onion
1/2 teaspoon salt
1/4 teaspoon paprika
1/4 teaspoon red (cayenne) pepper
1/2 teaspoon Italian seasoning

Place 1/2 cup butter or margarine in each of four separate small bowls. Add 1/2 cup flour to each bowl. Add a different seasoning to each bowl according to taste, choosing from remaining ingredients. Mix each thoroughly. Press mixture from each bowl into a 1-tablespoon measure. Slide out with a rubber spatula onto a baking sheet. Place in freezer until firm. When frozen, carefully place cubes that are alike in a plastic freezer bag. Label according to seasoning. To use frozen cubes, add 1 cube to 1/2 cup liquid. One cube plus 1/2 cup liquid makes 1/2 cup white sauce. Add additional cubes according to the amount of liquid. Makes 48 cubes.

Mayonnaise

Have ingredients at room temperature.

1 egg
1/4 teaspoon salt
2 tablespoons lemon juice
1 cup vegetable oil

Blend egg, salt, lemon juice and 1/4 cup oil in blender until mixture begins to thicken. If using blender, blend 2 minutes longer as you add remaining 3/4 cup oil. Pour oil in thin stream as you blend on low. If using an electric mixer, beat 3 to 5 minutes on medium-low. Beat until mixture is thick and smooth. Makes 1 cup.

Powdered Sugar

A quick way to make powdered sugar if you need it.

2 cups granulated sugar
2 tablespoons cornstarch

Place both ingredients in blender. Blend until fluffy. Turn blender off and on as you blend so you don't overheat motor. Makes 2-3/4 cups.

LOW-CALORIE SUBSTITUTIONS

When you want delicious meals that are nutritious and low in calories, try substituting foods. Check over the following list to find low-cal substitutes to save calories.

INSTEAD OF	TRY
Spaghetti	Bean sprouts French-cut green beans Spaghetti squash (a tasty low-calorie food)
Mayonnaise	Yogurt (especially good in salad dressings)

INSTEAD OF	TRY
Sour cream	Low-calorie imitation sour cream; plain, low-fat yogurt; low-fat cottage cheese, blended smooth
Whipped cream	Non-dairy topping; chilled evaporated milk (whipped)
Whole milk	Skim 2% or 1% butterfat milk, or nonfat dry milk (reconstituted)

EMERGENCY SUBSTITUTIONS

There's nothing worse than running out of a crucial ingredient in the middle of a recipe. If it happens to you, try one of these suggestions:

1 egg (for baking) =
two egg yolks or an egg-sized mound of mayonnaise

1 cup cake flour =
2 tablespoons cornstarch, then fill with all-purpose flour to one cup

1 teaspoon dry mustard =
1 tablespoon prepared mustard

1 cup butter or margarine =
1 cup shortening and 1/2 teaspoon salt

1 cup corn syrup =
1 cup sugar and 1/4 cup water

1 cup buttermilk =
1 cup milk and 1 tablespoon white vinegar

1 cup nuts =
1 cup Grapenuts cereal and 1/4 teaspoon almond flavoring

1 cup light cream =
1 cup undiluted evaporated milk

1 (15-oz.) can tomato sauce =
1 (6-oz.) can tomato paste and 3/4 cup water

1 tablespoon cornstarch (for thickening) =
2 tablespoons all-purpose flour

1 teaspoon baking powder =
1/2 teaspoon cream of tartar and 1/4 teaspoon baking soda

1 ounce unsweetened chocolate =
3 tablespoons cocoa powder and 1 tablespoon butter or margarine

1 cup molasses =
1 cup honey (taste is milder)

1 cup honey =
1-1/2 cups sugar and 1/4 cup water

1 cup sour cream (for baking) =
7/8 cup buttermilk and 3 tablespoons butter

1 cup heavy cream (for baking) =
1/3 cup melted butter or margarine and 3/4 cup milk

1 cup catsup or chili sauce =
1 cup tomato sauce, 1/4 cup sugar and 2 tablespoons vinegar

1 cup tomato paste =
1 cup tomato sauce plus 2 tablespoons all-purpose flour

COMMON DISASTERS

When disaster strikes, don't throw the food away. Try one of these fix-ups to save the day.

Scorched Stew—Use a wooden spoon to transfer unburned portion of stew into a different pan. Do not stir or scrape burned bottom. Add onion to help cover scorched flavor and water to prevent further scorching, if necessary.

Soggy, Overcooked Mashed Potatoes—Sprinkle with dry milk powder and powdered potatoes. Whip potatoes until smooth.

Other Scorches—Add a little sugar to mask taste.

Too Much Salt—Add lemon juice, vinegar or brown sugar. Add brown sugar or vinegar to beans. For large vegetables such as broccoli or cauliflower, rinse under running hot water. Discard water. Add small amount of fresh, unsalted water to rinsed vegetables. Cook until crisp-tender. For stew or soup, add wedges of raw potatoes. Discard when salt is absorbed.

Burned Rice—Place a crust of bread over the top of the rice. Cover and wait five minutes. Bread will reduce burned taste.

HOW MUCH IS ENOUGH?

When the recipe calls for a cup of sliced apples or a cup of bread crumbs or cracker crumbs, how do you know if you have enough? Here's a handy chart to help you.

1 cup fine cracker crumbs =
28 soda crackers

1/3 cup dry bread crumbs =
1 slice toast

**8 cups pared sliced apples
(or 5 to 6 cups applesauce) =**
3 pounds of apples

1 pound apples =
3 medium apples

1-1/4 cups chopped dates =
8 ounces pitted dates

1/4 to 1/3 cup orange juice =
juice of 1 large orange

1 cup grated Parmesan cheese =
3 ounces grated cheese

2-1/4 cups granulated sugar =
1 pound

2 cups cocoa =
8 ounces

4 cups cooked spaghetti =
8 ounces uncooked spaghetti

3 cups cooked noodles =
4 ounces uncooked noodles

2-1/2 cups + 2 tablespoons shortening =
1 pound

1 cup egg whites =
8 large egg whites

1/2 cup chopped onion =
1 medium onion, chopped

2/3 cup soft bread crumbs =
1 slice fresh bread

2-2/3 cups cut-up dried figs =
1 pound dried figs

1 cup chopped apple =
1 large apple, chopped

1-1/2 cups mashed bananas =
2 large bananas (1 pound)

2 to 3 tablespoons lemon =
juice of one lemon

2-1/4 cups cottage cheese =
1 pound

4 cups shredded Cheddar cheese =
1 pound

2-1/4 cups firmly packed brown sugar =
1 pound

2-1/2 cups chopped walnuts =
1 pound of shelled walnuts

8 cups cooked macaroni =
1 pound

6-3/4 cups cooked rice =
1 pound uncooked rice

1-1/4 cups catsup =
14 ounces

3/4 cup egg yolks =
8 egg yolks

4 cups all-purpose flour =
1 pound

30 TIDBITS FOR CREATIVE COOKS

1. If celery or carrots go limp before you use them, soak in cold water one hour. Add lemon juice or vinegar. Drain vegetables. Place in plastic bag and put in refrigerator until crisp.

2. For quick croutons, butter bread and sprinkle with spices such as sage, thyme, garlic salt or oregano. Cut into cubes and toast under broiler, stirring occasionally for even browning. Use in salads, soups or vegetables. Or use in dressings with meat.

3. To soften dried pastry, place in airtight container for 24 hours with slice of fresh bread.

4. Place hard brown sugar in airtight container with piece of fresh bread or apple slices. Wait 24 hours for sugar to soften.

5. Cookies too soft? Heat them in a 300F (150C) oven for five minutes. Too hard? Place in an air-tight container overnight with slice of fresh bread or apple slices.

6. Broil stale potato chips for a few minutes to restore freshness. Do not brown.

7. Place soggy crackers or cereal on baking sheet and heat a few minutes in the oven.

8. Grate hardened cheese for casseroles and pizza.

9. Before thawing old frozen vegetables, run boiling water over them. Drain all liquid and cook in fresh water. Add to soups or stews, or cook in broth.

10. If turkey tastes dry, sprinkle with water, cover with foil and heat. Serve with gravy over it.

11. For cream that will not whip, add an egg white and chill. Try again.

12. To tenderize tough meat or old stewing hen, marinate in equal amounts of vinegar and oil mixture. Let stand two hours, then drain liquid before cooking. Simmer slowly in water with few drops of vinegar. Cooking with moist heat will tenderize meat.

13. To remove tastes from deep-frying fat, fry potato slices until brown. Removes taste so you can use fat again.

14. To get maximum amount of juice from lemon, warm in water. Press down firmly and roll on hard surface before juicing.

15. Shake raisins or chopped dried fruit with some of the flour before adding to cake batter. It will keep them from sinking to bottom of cake.

16. Place unripe fruit in brown paper bag to speed ripening.

17. Place tomatoes in brown paper bag, pour boiling water over sack until bag breaks. Tomatoes will be ready to peel.

18. Cook potatoes in salt water for 10 minutes before baking. Shortens cooking time and saves energy.

19. Save orange-half by capping with plastic lid of appropriate size.

20. Save leftover vegetables in the freezer. When you've saved enough, use them in stews and soups.

21. Wrap fresh vegetables in damp paper towels and put in plastic bags before refrigerating. They'll last longer.

22. Chill meat or chicken before coating with flour. Coating sticks better. Or dip meat in slightly whipped egg white.

23. Use toasted dry bread, chopped in a blender, instead of flour to thicken casseroles.

24. Oatmeal or applesauce can stretch hamburger patties. Use one part applesauce or oatmeal to four parts hamburger.

25. Before opening a package of bacon, roll lengthwise back and forth into tube-shape with your hands. Slices loosen and separate easier when you open package.

26. For very thin slices of beef, slightly freeze beef before cutting. Cut slices across grain.

27. Empty leftover cereal or cookie crumbs into blender. Grind and store in airtight container. Use instead of graham crackers for tasty pie crust or dessert topping.

28. Break eggs into measuring cup before measuring shortening. Empty cup, then measure shortening. It won't stick.

29. To use last dribbles of catsup, put two tablespoons oil, one tablespoon vinegar and 1/8 teaspoon Italian seasoning in bottom of almost-empty bottle. Shake well and use as salad dressing.

30. Buy onions during harvest season. Put in old pantyhose leg, tying a knot between each onion. Hang in cool, dark place. Cut knot and onion will be ready to use.

Jane helps Dian put finishing touches on Pineapple Centerpiece.

Party Planning 2

PARTY SUCCESS

Good friends, good food and a well-organized party add up to a great time. This chapter is full of creative party tips and delicious recipes. It even includes a party planner to help you create a real memory-maker party.

PLANNING A PARTY

The forms at right and on the next page will help you organize and carry out a super party. Reproduce them on a copy machine or put them on a separate sheet of paper.

Overall Party Planner—This sheet is the beginning of your plans. Use it for general planning. Organize the type of party you want to have, the people you want to invite and the food and activities you desire.

Menu And Recipe Sheet—Use this to organize all food details. It tells where recipes can be found and the dishes to be served.

Shopping Planner—Everything to be purchased goes on this sheet. Food is categorized into sections to help you shop efficiently.

Party Checklist—Save time by listing things to do far ahead, several days ahead and the day of the party. Check off as you complete them.

OVERALL PARTY PLANNER

Type of Party _____

Date _____ Time _____

Location _____

GUEST LIST　　**Number of Guests** _____

Name　　Address　　Phone #　　RSVP

_____

_____

_____

_____

_____

_____

_____

_____

_____

Food or Activity Assignments _____

_____

General Comments (things to remember) _____

_____

_____

MENU AND RECIPE SHEET

Menu

Hors d'oeuvres _____

_____

Drinks _____

_____

Appetizer _____

_____

Salad _____

_____

Meat or Main Dish _____

_____

Vegetable _____

_____

Bread _____

_____

Dessert _____

_____

Condiments/Extras _____

_____

	Recipe	Book/Card	Page #
1.	_____		
2.	_____		
3.	_____		
4.	_____		
5.	_____		
6.	_____		
7.	_____		
8.	_____		
9.	_____		
10.	_____		

SHOPPING PLANNER

Fruits _____
Meats _____
Vegetables _____
Breads _____
Dairy Products _____
Canned Goods _____
Frozen Foods _____
Non-food Items _____

Paper Products _____
Flowers _____
Dishes _____
Linens Cleaned _____
Items For Activities _____
Film _____
Prizes _____
Other Errands _____

PARTY CHECKLIST

Check to be sure the following plans have been completed.

Far In Advance

____ 1. General party planning—theme, menu, activities, guest list, time and place.
____ 2. Invitations made and delivered.
____ 3. Complete detailed plans for menus, shopping lists and activities.

Several Days In Advance

____ 1. Finalize guest responses and assignments.
____ 2. Make any necessary revisions to party plans.
____ 3. Clean and prepare party area thoroughly.
____ 4. Prepare and freeze food (as many items as possible).
____ 5. Complete shopping trips (except perishables).

Day Of Party

____ 1. Tidy and touch-up party area.
____ 2. Decorate.
____ 3. Arrange tables and table settings.
____ 4. Shop for fresh food items.
____ 5. Last-minute check on details (enough ice and so forth).
____ 6. Plan time to get yourself ready.

Countdown To Party

Four hours before guests arrive: _____
Three hours: _____
Two hours: _____
One hour: _____
30 minutes: _____
Get-acquainted activities as guests arrive: _____

_____

Things To Schedule: _____

_____

NOVEL PARTY IDEAS

When you build your party around one creative idea, such as a clever theme or entertaining activity, your guests will remember it with pleasure long after the evening has ended. A novel theme or different activity makes your party a wonderful adventure. Before you know it, everyone is having a great time. This collection of party themes, activities, creations, cakes and unique tips will turn your party into a super success.

Give your party a great beginning by establishing a party theme. Food, decorations and clothes can all be part of the theme.

ANNIVERSARY PARTIES
Candlelight Dinner With A Different Flair—For a slightly zany celebration, borrow a flat-bed or pick-up truck. Take your partner to a drive-in movie. Set up a candlelight dinner for two in the truck bed and celebrate your anniversary with dinner and a movie.

Memory Treasure Hunt—Plan a treasure hunt down memory lane. Place clues at locations that mean something special to the couple. Clues may include the location of their first date, where the proposal took place and so on. Each clue can be a verse expressing what that location means to the honored couple. It should lead to the next location on the treasure hunt. Clues lead to a special gift or a restaurant or home where the celebration will occur.

PARTY IDEAS AND CREATIONS
Guess-Who Party—When guests arrive, give each a questionnaire to fill out. Questions should require short answers. Guests turn in questionnaires to the host or hostess without discussing answers with other guests. Host or hostess reads each questionnaire aloud. Each guest writes down the name of the person he thinks completed it. Guests with the most correct and least correct answers win prizes.

Sample Questionnaire
1. If you could go anywhere in the world, where would it be?
2. Who would you take with you to a desert island?
3. What is your favorite food?
4. Favorite color?
5. Favorite car?
6. Favorite movie?
7. Favorite sport?
8. Favorite recording artist(s)?
9. Favorite saying or quotation?
10. World leader you would like to change places with?

Hot Bread Party—Ask each friend to bring a loaf of favorite bread. Have yours in the oven ready to serve as guests arrive. Serve breads warm with cheese, honey, jams and whipped butter.

Letter Party—If your favorite person's friends are scattered, throw a letter party to honor his birthday. Send a postcard to friends asking each to send a card or letter with an appropriate message to honor your friend. Have them send letters to you in advance so all cards arrive before the party or birthday. Deliver the cards to the person on his special day.

Pineapple Centerpiece—Use a beautiful fresh pineapple for a centerpiece. Stand it on a tray and cover pineapple with pineapple chunks and maraschino cherries speared with toothpicks. As the party progresses, pull out the toothpicks and eat the pineapple and cherries. Bring out the cutting board and knife. Cut the pineapple into wedges and eat it too!

Lunar Schooner—This creation will delight your guests. You'll need a glass brandy snifter and a nesting bowl that protrudes out of the top of the snifter. Fill the snifter half-full with water. Color water with food coloring. Drop small chunks of dry ice in water just before serving.

Place cold sherbet or ice cream in glass dish. Spoon on topping if desired. Nest in top of snifter. Dry ice "fog" will create a misty atmosphere.

Cassette Scavenger Hunt—Divide guests into teams. List 10 to 20 sounds each group must record. Examples are police-car siren, bird call, cash register ringing, music from a record and so on. Assign points to each sound according to how difficult it is to find. Give each team a portable cassette tape recorder and blank cassette tape for recording. Send teams off with a time to report back. Team with the most points wins.

Chocolate Leaves For Cake Decorating—Gather 20 to 30 rose leaves from your garden (or obtain from florist). Wash thoroughly and dry leaves. Melt an 8-oz. milk chocolate candy bar in double boiler. Lay waxed paper on a baking sheet or hold leaf in hand. With a knife, spatula or paint brush, put chocolate on the underneath side of each leaf. Put baking sheet in the refrigerator. When chocolate has hardened, remove rose leaves. Place chocolate leaves in a storage container in refrigerator and use as garnish. Pastel chocolate can also be used.

Gelatin Mold Punch Rings—Using different-shaped gelatin molds, freeze a portion of your party punch ahead of time. Place ice ring in your punch bowl.

Apple-Candle Centerpiece—Using an apple corer, core five or six large apples. Place tall, thin candles in the core of each apple. Arrange with fall leaves for fall decor or green and red bows in evergreen boughs for Christmas.

Sombrero Spread

A different dip.

2 (16-oz.) cans chili-with-meat
2 (16-oz.) cans refried beans
1/2 lb. Cheddar cheese, grated
2 tomatoes, diced
5 to 7 green onions, chopped
1/4 cup sliced olives
2 (10-oz.) pkgs. taco chips

Mix chili and refried beans together. Heat in saucepan. Pour into round chafing dish. Arrange cheese on top of beans in a circle around outside. Put tomatoes in a circle inside cheese, then onions, finishing with olives in middle. Serve as dip with taco chips.

Grape Ice Cubes—When you see grapes in the grocery store at a reasonable price, pick up several extra bunches. Wash, remove stems and freeze in ice-cube trays in punch or water. For your next party, use grape cubes in glass or punch bowl.

Crockpot Server-Warmer—Use your crockpot to keep drinks warm at your next party. Put cider or spicy punch in crockpot. Turn on low. Keep lid on for very hot beverages or leave lid off for warm beverages.

Serve Food In Food—If you want to do something unusual for a party, serve food in food. Try the following ideas.

- Cream cheese in cherry tomatoes.
- Vegetable dip in a cabbage.
- Shrimp-cream cheese mixture in a tomato.
- Cream-of-chicken soup in hubbard squash.
- Pumpkin soup in a pumpkin.
- Meatloaf in an onion.
- Rice casserole in acorn squash.
- Chili in red or green peppers.
- Quiche in summer squash.
- Fruit salad in watermelon.
- Shrimp salad in cantaloupe.
- Gelatin cubes in an orange.
- Fruit and nut salad in an avocado.
- Baked Alaska in an orange.
- Chili in a round loaf of bread.
- Yogurt and fruit in a honeydew melon.

Instant Garbage Can—If you need an extra garbage can for a party or clean-up, use the metal stand from a TV tray that has a leg brace. Place large plastic bag on stand. Bag hangs in middle of stand, where tray would be. Fold top of bag over metal-tube top of stand so it is open and ready to use.

GIFTS
GIFTS
GIFTS
GIFTS
GIFTS
GIFTS

Everyone enjoys presents. Gifts can express best wishes, friendship, esteem or love. With a little thought and imagination, your gifts can bring you more joy and give more delight to the receiver. The following ideas will add creativity to your gift-giving.

- Tie dollar bills to a branch with red ribbon for an instant money tree.
- Wrap your present with another gift. Tie a jumprope around a child's gift. Wrap a kitchen gift in a hand towel.
- Fill up a friend's car with gas.
- Include extra stamps when writing to someone special.
- Put jelly in an attractive drinking mug. Seal jelly with wax and tie a ribbon around the mug.
- Give a roll of dimes or quarters to a hospital patient as a get-well gift. The money will come in handy for all sorts of small things.
- Give coupons for such items as a date to a movie, a night's free babysitting or a special event the recipient and you can share.
- Give a roll of stamps to a newlywed or college student.
- Give a hammer, saw, wheelbarrow or other tool as a wedding, shower or housewarming gift.
- If you need a last-minute gift for a child's birthday party, put money in balloons. Blow them up and tie together. Or tie money to balloon strings.

- Tie several money-filled balloons on dowels and stick them in a flowerpot with leaves. It's a money bouquet!
- Pay the first-year's rent on a safety deposit box for someone who has just moved.
- Give an elderly person an "unbirthday" gift by bringing in dinner. Set the table with candles and special dinnerware. Seat guests and serve dinner. Leave kitchen spotless.
- Give grandmother a photo album with the first page filled with your family pictures. As you take pictures throughout the year, send a copy to her for her album.
- Buy a tree for a friend and help plant it.
- Give 12 days of Christmas to a special friend. Each night leave an inexpensive gift anonymously. On the 12th day take your gift in person and enjoy the surprise.
- For a perfect child's gift, fill the back of a toy dumptruck with fresh-baked muffins, cookies or other treats. Cover with plastic wrap and a colorful bow.

CHILD'S PARTY IDEAS

A child's party can be one of the most important parties you plan all year. To delight and entertain small guests, you'll need to plan everything very carefully to create a fun time. These ideas will help you use your talents to make your next little people's party the best ever!

CHILD'S PARTY FOODS AND ACTIVITIES

Snowball Caterpillar—Arrange snowball cupcakes to form body of a caterpillar. Attach red or black licorice sticks to side of each cupcake for legs. Use two gumdrops for eyes and two pipe cleaners topped with gumdrops for antennae.

Variation: Line up tomatoes and use olives for eyes and black pipe cleaners for legs. Cream puffs can be stuffed with sandwich filling and arranged the same way.

Fruit Totem Pole—Purchase a honeydew melon, several different fruits, a dowel and a 2-foot cord. Put honeydew melon on bottom of totem pole. Lay cord snugly around bottom of melon to keep it from rolling or place in wooden bowl. Insert dowel in melon. Slip fruit onto dowel. Decorate fruit with paper faces and symbols.

Cupcake Numbers—When a number is part of your celebration, make it with cupcakes. Bake and frost cupcakes. On tray or table, place cupcakes side by side, forming shape of the number. If the occasion is a birthday, each cupcake may have a candle inserted and lit.

Ice-Block Slides—Ice-block slides can make your party exciting. Buy 3 to 4 frozen ice blocks from supermarket or ice company. Give each guest an old bath towel. Use grass-covered hills with no trees or rocks in the path of sliders. Divide into as many teams as you have blocks of ice. Slide down hills with towel on top of ice block to keep seats dry. Adult supervision keeps this activity safe and fun. For children 8 to 15.

Lifesaver Candleholders—Use Lifesavers as holders for candles on a birthday cake. Lifesavers catch wax drippings better than plastic candle holders and make a colorful addition to birthday decor.

Decorate The Tablecloth—Cover the party table with plain white butcher paper. Mark off sections and write each child's name at his place. Using crayons or markers, let each child create his own design.

Stencil Cake—On a piece of waxed cardboard (such as a TV dinner carton), draw a simple silhouette. Children enjoy animal shapes such as a teddy bear.

Cut silhouette shape from cardboard with razor blade or knife. Frost cake and let it stand a few hours. Place stencil, waxed side down, on frosted cake. Make contrasting color frosting. Spread over edges of stencil and cake from top of stencil to bottom. Lift stencil from cake. Second or contrasting layer of frosting will form silhouette on top of cake. Decorate as desired.

Balloon Cake—Decorate frosted layer cake with gumdrop balloons. You will need 15 to 20 flat, round, fruit-flavored gumdrops. Cut end of gumdrop off to give balloon a bright fresh color. Arrange on cake. Add short strands of black or red shoestring licorice for strings on each candy balloon.

To make cake an exciting centerpiece, anchor strings of one or more colorful helium-filled balloons around it. Or use a Bundt-shaped cake and anchor strings to center of cake.

Flowerpot Cake—You'll need an unglazed clay flowerpot, drinking straw, dowel, foil and some colorful cardboard to make this attractive cake. Line pot with large pieces of foil. This will make removal of cake easier.

Pour cake batter into flowerpot, filling 2/3 full. Insert straw vertically into middle of batter so cake will vent and rise. Clip straw 1 to 2 inches above cake batter before baking. Bake until you can pull straw out without batter.

Frost top of cake with chocolate icing or crushed chocolate cookies. Draw colorful flower on posterboard or use a large tissue-paper or crepe-paper flower. Write appropriate message on flower and attach to wooden dowel. Secure dowel upright in cake.

Flowerpot Ice-Cream Cake—Pack foil-lined flowerpot with chocolate-almond-fudge ice cream. Sprinkle crushed dark-chocolate cookies on top. Put in freezer. Add flower when ready to serve.

For individual portions, use a paper cup or small pot for a flowerpot. Freeze ahead. When ready to serve, sprinkle with crushed cookies, attach flower to end of spoon handle and place spoon upright in ice cream.

CHILD'S PARTY FAVORS

Orange Edible Favor—Have each child color a jack-o-lantern face on an orange with a black marker. If it's spring, draw a bunny face and add construction paper ears. Each child takes his creation home with him to eat.

Photo Favor—Take an instant photo of each child at the party. When it's time to go home, give each child his picture to take with him to remember the fun.

Cookies-On-A-Stick—Make a clever favor or cake decoration by placing a wooden ice cream stick in a thick sugar cookie before baking. Cookie can be eaten easily, without mess. Children can decorate cookie with icing and candies.

THEME PARTIES FOR CHILDREN

Backyard Circus Party—Guests at this party are the entertainment. Each child is invited to dress as a circus performer. Clown-face invitations might say, "Come one, come all to the backyard circus!" Message inside explains that each party-goer should come dressed as a circus character and includes date, time and place of the party.

Backyard decorations are the key to this party. Hang a sign at the entrance: "Welcome to the Backyard Circus!" As each child arrives, letter sign with child's name. Indicate the performer or act he is portraying. A picnic table becomes the snack bar where you serve popcorn, punch and ice-cream cones.

Children may come dressed as characters they choose or you can suggest costumes for each one. Some ideas include:

- **Tightrope act**—Use a 2x4 board to walk on.
- **Strongman**—To make barbells, use a cardboard tube with balloons on each end. Write "1000 pounds" on each balloon.
- **Acrobat or baton girl**—Use wooden dowels for batons.
- **Ringmaster**—Ask a child to come dressed in a scaled-down version of "coat and tails."
- **Clown**—Children dressed as clowns could do tricks.

As the party progresses, each performer takes a turn on stage. As each finishes, present the child with a party favor such as a balloon filled with helium.

Indian Birthday Party—Using shapes and symbols from American Indian culture, create an Indian Birthday Party. From brown paper bags cut teepees for invitations. Let birthday child color and design each one. Write information inside.

Make an Indian vest and headband for each guest from paper grocery bags. Cut off bottom of bag. Cut open center, lay sack flat and fold ends over like a vest. Cut out neck, large armholes and round front and back. Fringe bottom and tape shoulders. Make headband and insert feather. Let children decorate vests and headbands during party.

Bake a rectangular cake. Cut it into a teepee-shape and frost. Send guests home with their colorful Indian vests and headbands.

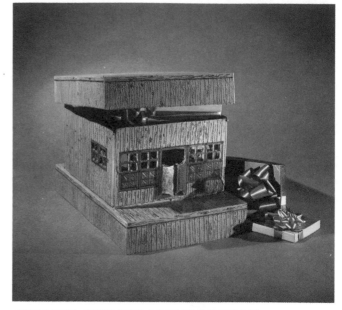

Pirate Birthday Party—As each child arrives, wrap a colorful sash around his waist. Tie a black construction-paper eyepatch connected to string around his head. Hang an earring over his ear. Make earring by tying short string in a circle with small canning ring hanging from it.

Top each head with newspaper pirate hat. Follow steps in diagrams below.

For a pirate activity, draw a treasure map with footsteps to clues or small treasures around the house and yard. At first stop, treasure could be a drawstring cloth bag to hold small gifts and favors. Last stop could be all the birthday presents. If guests vary in age and ability, arrange clues to individual treasures or hide harder-to-find treasures for older children and easier-to-find treasures for smaller guests.

CHILD'S GIFTWRAPPING IDEAS

Using household objects, a picture and a touch of creativity, make one of these surprises.

Old Saloon Giftwrapping—Having a cowboy party? Place gifts inside a cardboard-box saloon. Guests might be invited to bring cowboy-type gifts, such as toy horses, cowboy and Indian people, hats, chaps and guns.

To make a saloon gift-holder, find a picture of a saloon in a book or use above photo as a guide. Get 3 cardboard boxes, 2 shirt-type boxes and 1 heavy, taller cardboard box with a lid. One shirt box is the porch and one is the roof. The heavier, taller box is the main building.

Tape shirt boxes onto building box. Paint brown. Using black marker, draw swinging bar doors and shutter windows. With a knife, cut open doors and windows. Tape small cowboy figures on porch and stand horses in front.

PIRATE HAT

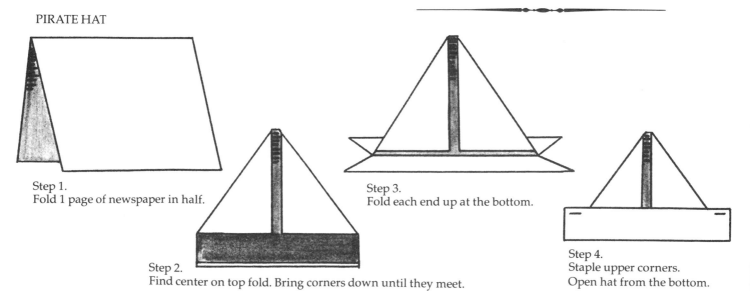

Step 1.
Fold 1 page of newspaper in half.

Step 2.
Find center on top fold. Bring corners down until they meet.

Step 3.
Fold each end up at the bottom.

Step 4.
Staple upper corners.
Open hat from the bottom.

Steam-Engine Giftwrapping—What a surprise for your child to find all of his gifts hidden in a black steam engine. To make this steam engine, find a coloring-book picture of an old locomotive or use above picture as a guide. Collect paper tubes from paper towels and a variety of cardboard boxes for the engine.

Tape tubes and boxes together with masking tape to form the engine. Attach wheels cut from heavy cardboard and spray engine black. Put gifts in engine so it is easy for child to get them out. He may want to keep locomotive for future play.

Scarecrow Giftwrapping—If you're having a warm-weather fall party, make a Wizard of Oz scarecrow. Stuff old shirt, pants, shoes, gloves and hat with newspaper. Make head out of nylon stocking stuffed with cotton batting. Stitch a mouth and nose to form the face. See photo.

Put hat on head and stuff straw around gloves and shoes. Hide child's gifts in pockets and inside hat. Or arrange gifts around pumpkins. Place scarecrow in corner of yard with a pumpkin for each guest. Have each child make a jack-o-lantern face on his pumpkin with black marker. Children can take home jack-o-lantern pumpkins as favors.

Dian and Tom Brokaw mix up Winter Picnic thermos recipes.

Picnics

Family picnics are great! They get the whole family outdoors in the fresh air, enjoying food together. Each member of the family should participate in planning and creating a unique experience for all to enjoy.

You can plan a picnic in the winter, as well as summer. Have a picnic at a park, on the ski slopes, in your backyard, even around your fireplace!

This chapter will help you make the most of your next picnic. Use the ideas, change them, rearrange them. Be creative! And have a good time.

SUMMERTIME PICNICS

Look around your house when planning a family get-together or a backyard picnic party. You can transform household items into unusual party accessories.

Wheelbarrow Party-Server—Line wheelbarrow with plastic and fill with ice. It is ideal for serving salads and canned pop. Wheelbarrow can be rolled to a convenient, shady spot for serving. Ice will keep drinks and salads cool.

Permanent Picnic Tablecloth—Attach artificial grass with short nap to worn-out picnic table. It washes off easily with a hose and is always ready for a picnic.

Windproof Tablecloth—Make your tablecloth windproof by adding special pockets to it. Stitch pockets with sections to hold paper plates, napkins and flatware. Drapery weights can be attached to the hem to keep ends from blowing into food. See diagram at right for pattern.

Insect-Proof Salad Serving—Stretch plastic wrap in embroidery hoops. Use as covers over salads and other foods. Food is protected from insects and clear wrap lets guests see what's inside.

Too Many Insects—Use two electric fans, one on each side of picnic table, to keep insects away from food. Keep plates and cups weighted down with food and liquid so they don't fly away, too!

Pineapple Boat—Serve fresh pineapple in an easy, elegant way. Cut pineapple in quarters lengthwise. Do not remove outside rind or crown. Remove core from each quarter. Using crescent-shaped grapefruit knife, slice each quarter between fruit and rind to detach fruit. Leave rind intact. Slice fruit vertically, leaving it in pineapple. Place on plates.

Slightly push each section in alternating directions. Skewer maraschino cherries on toothpicks in each pineapple piece. Makes 4 boats.

Ironing-Board Buffet—Change your ironing board into a portable serving table. Keep it from tipping by placing sandbags over the bar or putting bricks against the legs. Cover it with a decorative tablecloth. Arrange plates, cups and flatware so people can pick them up as they go through the buffet line.

Watermelon Fruit-Salad Server—Slice watermelon in half horizontally. Use an ice-cream scoop to scoop out good-size cups from surface of a watermelon. Fill each scooped-out cup with different kinds of fresh fruit. Place a fruit dip in one cup. Provide toothpicks so guests can select their favorite fruits and enjoy the dip. When fruit is gone, use a melon baller to scoop out remaining watermelon.

SUMMER TREATS

Cool it on a hot summer day! These refreshing summer foods will make a hit as a snack or mealtime delight for children and adults.

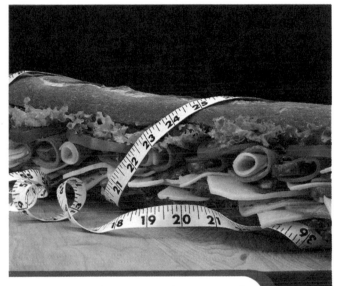

Sandwich By-The-Inch

Let guests cut servings to match appetites.

2 (12-inch) loaves French bread, unsliced
1/3 cup butter or margarine, softened
1/2 cup mayonnaise
1 tablespoon prepared mustard
16 slices luncheon meat
16 slices cheese
4 tomatoes, sliced
Shredded lettuce
Dill pickle, sliced thin

Slice each loaf in half lengthwise. Butter each half. Combine mayonnaise and mustard in a small bowl. Spread on buttered bread. Layer 8 slices meat and 8 slices cheese on 1/2 of each loaf. Arrange tomato slices over cheese. Top with shredded lettuce and pickles. Place top of loaf over pickles, making foot-long sandwiches. Have guests cut off desired portions. Serves 6 to 12.

Refreshing Fruit Pizza

A beautiful sight to behold!

1 (15-oz.) can pineapple chunks
3 bananas
1 (15-oz.) pkg. sugar-cookie mix
1 (8-oz.) container whipped topping —
1 (10-1/2-oz.) can mandarin oranges, drained
2 cups sliced fresh strawberries
1/2 cup cherry pie-filling
1 kiwi fruit

use my almond sugar cookie dough recipe

instead use cream cheese + powdered sugar mixture Yum!

Drain juice from pineapple chunks into a small bowl. Slice bananas into juice; set aside. Preheat oven to 375F (190C). Prepare cookie dough according to package directions. Lightly grease a 12-inch pizza pan. Press dough into pizza pan, about 1/8-inch thick. Bake 12 to 15 minutes or until edges begin to brown. Cool on a rack.

Spread whipped topping over cooled cookie-dough crust. Drain juice from bananas. Arrange fruit in circles on topping, working from outside toward center. Arrange strawberries around outside of pan, then bananas, cherry pie-filling, pineapple chunks and mandarin oranges. Place a whole strawberry in center. Refrigerate until served. Create your own fresh-fruit combinations. Serves 8.

Vegetable Dip

Nutritious treat that's quick to make.

1 pt. plain yogurt
1 (1-1/4-oz.) pkg. ranch-style dressing mix

Season yogurt to taste with dressing mix. Combine ingredients in a plastic or glass container. Shake well. Use as a dip with vegetables or over salads as dressing. Try it with baked potatoes, too! Makes 2 cups.

Ham Roll-Up

Great ham-and-cheese combo.

1 (8-oz.) pkg. ham, sliced
1 (8-oz.) pkg. cream cheese, softened
1 bunch green onions

Spread cream cheese on slices of ham. Lay green onion along the edge of ham. Roll. Chill until cream cheese is firm, then slice. Serves 4 to 6.

Party Onions

These tasty treats vanish quickly.

1 tablespoon milk
1 (3-oz.) pkg. cream cheese
1 bunch small green onions (8 to 12)
1-1/2 cups shredded sharp Cheddar cheese,
**   room temperature**

Blend milk into cream cheese in a small bowl; set aside. Wash and trim onions. Cover white onion bulbs with cream cheese mixture. Roll coated bulbs in Cheddar cheese. Serves 4 to 6.

Dilly Dip

A dilly of a dressing.

1 cup dairy sour cream
1-1/2 tablespoons minced onion
1 cup mayonnaise
1 tablespoon chopped parsley
1-1/2 tablespoons dill
1 tablespoon Beau Monde seasoning

Combine ingredients in a glass jar or plastic container and shake well. Terrific with cold vegetables. Try with hot vegetables for unique taste treat. Makes 2 cups.

Fruit Pudding Refresher

For an extra treat, serve this salad in a flowerpot!

1 (20-oz.) can pineapple chunks in juice
2 bananas, sliced
1 cup shredded coconut
1 (11-oz.) can mandarin oranges, drained
1 (16-oz.) can fruit cocktail with juice
1 (3-3/4-oz.) pkg. instant lemon pudding mix

In medium bowl, combine pineapple chunks and juice with bananas, oranges, fruit cocktail with juice and coconut. Stirring slowly, sprinkle pudding mix into fruit mixture. Let stand 5 minutes. Pudding will set in fruit juice. Makes 6-1/2 cups.

Tin-Can Ice Cream

Ice cream without an ice-cream maker!

1 cup milk   **1 egg (optional)**
1 cup whipping cream
1/2 cup sugar
1/2 teaspoon vanilla extract
Nuts or fruit as desired

Put all ingredients in a 1-pound coffee can with a tight-fitting plastic lid. Place lid on can. Place can with ingredients inside a #10 can with a tight-fitting plastic lid.

Pack larger can with crushed ice around smaller can. Pour at least 3/4 cup of rock salt evenly over ice. Place lid on #10 can. Roll back and forth on a table or cement slab for 10 minutes. Open outer can. Remove inner can with ingredients. Remove lid. Use a rubber spatula to stir up mixture; scrape sides of can. Replace lid. Drain ice water from larger can. Insert smaller can; pack with more ice and salt. Roll back and forth for five more minutes. Makes about 3 cups.

Frozen Fruit Pops

Make your own fruit pops.

1 (28-oz.) can fruit of any kind, drained
1/4 cup corn syrup, light or dark
Paper cups
Wooden ice-cream sticks

Purée drained fruit and corn syrup in blender. Fill paper cups with purée. Small 4-ounce cups work well for small children. Larger cups such as 6- or 8-ounce size satisfy bigger appetites. Insert a stick in center of each cup. Place in freezer until firm. Peel off cup to serve. Serves 4 to 6.

Pineapple Pops

A nutritious treat.

1 (20-oz.) can pineapple slices
6 wooden ice-cream sticks
6 maraschino cherries

Place six pineapple slices on a baking sheet. Push stick through the center of a maraschino cherry until at least 1/2 inch of the stick shows on top. Lay stick across pineapple slice so cherry is in center of slice. Place another slice of pineapple on top and freeze. When frozen, place each piece in a plastic freezer bag or wrap in plastic freezer wrap until ready to eat. Serves 6.

Frozen Bananas On A Stick

A super-delicious banana.

3 bananas
6 wooden ice-cream sticks
1 cup orange juice
1 cup milk-chocolate pieces
2 tablespoons vegetable oil
3/4 cup chopped peanuts, optional
3/4 cup shredded coconut, optional

Cover baking sheet with waxed paper; set aside. Slice peeled bananas in half crosswise and insert stick. Dip into orange juice. Place in freezer until firm. Melt chocolate pieces and vegetable oil in top of double boiler. Spoon melted chocolate evenly over bananas. Chocolate will harden fast, so work rapidly. Roll coated bananas in chopped peanuts or shredded coconut. Serve immediately or wrap in plastic wrap and freeze. Serves 6.

Pudding On A Stick

Smooth and refreshing.

1 (3-3/4-oz.) pkg. instant pudding, any flavor
2 cups cold milk
Wooden ice-cream sticks

Whip pudding and milk in medium bowl until mixture begins to thicken. Pour into paper cups. Place a stick in the cup. Place in freezer until firm. Serves 4 to 6.

WINTER FUN

Why not have a picnic in January? It's fun to enjoy winter's outdoor beauty and eat a warm tasty meal while you're skiing, ice skating, building a snowman or sculpting ice.

THERMOS RECIPES

These winter treats are especially tasty on a cold day!

Hot Chili—A meal of steaming chili is a favorite warmer-upper. Keep chili warm in thermos while you play in the snow. One secret to delicious, hearty chili is coarsely ground beef instead of regular hamburger. Ask your butcher for coarsely ground stew beef or round steak.

Chili Dogs On A Bun—For a treat, try a hot dog with chili in a thermos. Tie a 12-inch length of dental floss around hot dog and heat in saucepan with chili. Lower hot dog into thermos with string hanging out the top. Pour chili around hot dog and cap thermos. Use end of floss to pull hot dog from chili into bun. Pull floss through dog and spoon chili onto bun for a delicious chili dog.

Hot Chili Chips In A Bag—Take along individual corn-chip bags or put chips in self-sealing bags. Open bag and pour hot chili from thermos over chips. Bring along plastic spoon and enjoy chili chips in a bag. A great idea for football games on a cold day.

Hot Chicken In Noodle Soup—Serve another treat using chicken and chicken-noodle soup. Tie dental floss or string around the end of a hot, cooked chicken drumstick. Lower chicken into thermos. Fill thermos with hot chicken-noodle soup.

OTHER OUTDOOR WINTER TREATS

These treats will fill you up and keep you warm.

Hot Chicken Loaf

Take a hot chicken sandwich to a ball game or picnic.

8 chicken thighs
1/2 cup all-purpose flour
1/4 cup vegetable oil
6 green onions, chopped
1/4 pound fresh mushrooms, sliced
1 (16-oz.) jar spaghetti sauce
1 (12- to 14-inch) loaf French bread

Grease a 7-1/2x12" baking dish; set aside. Preheat oven to 350F (175C). Roll chicken thighs in flour. In a medium skillet, brown floured chicken thighs in oil then place in baking dish. Mix onions, mushrooms and spaghetti sauce in medium bowl. Spoon over chicken thighs. Bake 20 minutes until bubbly. Cut top quarter off French bread, lengthwise. Hollow out center of loaf, leaving 1/2-inch crust. Remove bones from chicken thighs by holding both ends with pieces of foil to protect fingers. Twist bone to separate it from meat. It will come out easily. Discard bones. Use fork to arrange boned chicken thighs in hollow center of bread loaf. Spoon sauce over chicken. Cover with top slice of bread. Wrap loaf in foil. Place on baking sheet and bake 20 minutes. Serve immediately or later. If loaf will be eaten later, wrap newspaper around it. Serve within 45 minutes. Serves 4 or 5.

Fruit Leather Snacks—If you're looking for a quick sweet-treat while snowshoeing or cross-country skiing, fruit leather may be just the ticket.

To make fruit leather, purée fresh fruit or drained canned fruit in a blender. Add 1 tablespoon of lemon juice or ascorbic acid to each quart of fresh fruit.

Cover inverted baking sheet with heat-resistant plastic wrap. (As shown in photo above.) Tape wrap to baking sheet with masking tape. This prevents edges from pulling up while fruit is drying. Pour purée about 1/4-inch thick over baking sheet. Leave about 1 inch free of fruit around the edge.

Dry in a food dryer or in an oven at 140F (60C) with oven door open at least 2 inches. Dry until purée is leathery but still pliable and not sticky to the touch. Takes several hours.

Roll up leather and store in an airtight container. When you're hungry, unroll fruit and eat.

Your Own Hot Box—Cook a hot meal while skating, skiing or driving to an outdoor picnic. Make a *hot box*—a newspaper-lined cardboard box. Before leaving, prepare your favorite stew, chili, spaghetti or other hearty one-dish meal in a cast-iron Dutch oven or aluminum pressure cooker. Cook dish 2/3 to 3/4 of the recommended cooking time. While dish is cooking, line an appropriate-size box or Styrofoam container with at least 1 inch of newspaper on all sides. Take pot directly from oven or stove and place in lined box. Add more papers around and over box so Dutch oven or kettle fits snugly in papers. Close box. Food will continue to cook and stay warm for several hours.

FIREPLACE AND WINTER COOKING

A fireplace adds warmth and romance to any gathering. But it can also be used for cooking. Fireplace cooking saves fuel, provides entertainment for family or friends and furnishes dinner all at the same time.

The Fire—Fireplace cooking demands a good, steady fire that will burn down to enough coals for cooking. Make sure you have enough wood, from tinder to fuel.

Tinder is small, burnable material used to start the fire. Pieces of paper, leaves, small twigs, shavings or bark make good tinder. Make your own firestarting tinder from cardboard egg cartons. Fill each compartment with clothes-dryer lint. Pour melted paraffin over material in each compartment. Cut off one compartment and nest in kindling. Light the cardboard compartment. Waxed material should burn long and hot enough to start wood. Or use a piece of pressed log. Cut off a 2-inch piece, place it among kindling and light. One log starts many fires.

Kindling is larger than tinder and catches fire fairly easily. It feeds the fire until it is hot enough to burn larger pieces of wood. Kindling ranges from pencil-size to 2 to 3 inches in diameter.

Fuel is larger pieces of wood, usually 3 to 4 inches in diameter to large logs. It burns down to provide coals for cooking. A good cooking fire requires enough fuel to provide a large pile of coals. Hardwoods such as oak, mahogany, fruitwood and mesquite burn longer and cleaner than softwoods such as pine or fir.

Building A Cooking Fire—Plan to let a good fire burn 15 to 20 minutes to provide enough coals for cooking. Arrange kindling and tinder and light them. Add more kindling. Finally, add fuel wood, arranging it so air circulates around each piece. If fire smolders, fan with a paper plate or bellows to provide more oxygen. Cover hearth with extra-heavy foil to protect it from drips.

Don't try to cook over a roaring fire. Intense heat causes food to char on the outside and remain raw on the inside. Let fuel burn until hot, glowing coals remain. Coals provide an even heat to cook food all the way through.

Regulating Heat—You can cook almost anything using heat from your fireplace. All you need to learn is how to regulate the temperature. If you're grilling, boiling or frying, regulate temperature by raising or lowering the rack on which you rest your foods. An oven rack propped on bricks works well. Add more bricks to lower temperature.

SPECIAL TOOLS TO ADD VERSATILITY

Shovel Grill—If you need a solid grill for frying hamburgers, cover the top of a clean shovel with heavy-duty foil. Prop it over cooking coals. Long handle helps you take tool off heat without burning your fingers.

Dutch Oven Baking—Use a heavy cast-iron Dutch oven in your fireplace for warming foods, cooking soups and stews, and roasting meats. This versatile tool will also bake pies, cakes and biscuits. A Dutch oven with legs to hold it above coals serves as an ideal fireplace tool. You can achieve the same effect by propping a legless Dutch oven on bricks.

To bake a pie in your fireplace, place 3 canning-jar rings or 3 flat rocks about 1/2-inch high in a Dutch oven. Put pie pan on rings or rocks so warmed air can circulate around it. Place Dutch oven 1 inch above cooking coals. With tongs or a shovel, put hot coals on lid of Dutch oven. If oven does not have flat lid with a lip to hold coals, make a collar of foil around lid. Bake until done.

Try the following delightful recipes. Your family and friends will never believe you cooked them in the fireplace.

Upside-Down Cake In A Dutch Oven

A treat to cook and eat!

1 (16-oz.) can pineapple slices
2 tablespoons butter or margarine
1 (8-oz.) jar maraschino cherries
1/2 cup packed brown sugar
1 (18-1/2-oz.) pkg. cake mix

Drain fruit, reserving pineapple juice. Line Dutch oven with foil. Grease foil. Arrange pineapple with cherries in center of each slice on top of foil. Sprinkle brown sugar and 3 tablespoons of reserved juice over fruit. Prepare cake mix according to package directions. Pour over fruit. Put cover on Dutch oven.

To bake, place in fireplace 1 inch above coals. Legs of oven should keep bottom of oven 1 inch above coals. If oven does not have legs, place on bricks. Use tongs or shovel to arrange coals on top of the Dutch oven. Bake 25 to 30 minutes or until a toothpick inserted in center of cake comes out clean. Cool 8 minutes in pan, then invert onto platter. Carefully peel away foil.

You can adapt conventional casserole recipes to Dutch-oven cooking. The tasty dish on the next page will please anyone who likes hamburger casseroles with a south-of-the-border flavor.

Enchilada Pie

A super supper.

2 lbs. ground beef
1 teaspoon salt
1 medium onion, chopped
1 (10-3/4-oz.) can condensed tomato soup
2 (10-oz.) cans mild enchilada sauce
1 cup water
9 (8-inch) flour tortillas
2 cups shredded sliced Cheddar or
  mozarella cheese (8 oz.)

Working over an open fire, brown ground beef with salt and onion in a Dutch oven. Drain off drippings. Add condensed soup, enchilada sauce and water. Simmer 5 minutes. Spoon 3/4 of the mixture into a medium bowl.

Arrange 2 to 3 tortillas over mixture remaining in pan. Alternate meat, cheese and tortillas in 3 layers. Replace lid on Dutch oven. Simmer 7 to 10 minutes or until cheese melts and tortillas soften. Serve pie with remaining tortillas as side bread. Serves 6 to 8.

Foil Cooking—Foil-wrapped food can be cooked on racks 1 to 2 inches above coals. Many different foods are delicious cooked in foil.

For foil cooking, lay foil dinners directly on rack, about 1 inch above coals. Do the same for foil-wrapped potatoes. Broiled foods, such as steak or hamburger, and foods you want to fry or warm quickly, should be elevated about 3 to 4 inches from the coals. Larger cuts of meat and other foods that need cooking for long periods should also be elevated farther from the coals.

Reflector Ovens—A camper's reflector oven can bake many treats in front of a fireplace. It's one of the few methods of cooking in which flames are used to cook food. Heat from flames reflects off shiny sides of the oven and cooks food placed on a rack. One advantage of this technique over Dutch-oven baking is that you can tell immediately whether foods are baking too quickly or too slowly. Increase temperature by moving oven closer to the flames or decrease it by moving oven farther away. Cookies, pizza and rolls are delicious baked in a reflector oven.

Banana Boat.

Cake In Orange Cups

Bake your cake in the coals, too!

12 to 18 oranges
1 (18-1/2-oz.) pkg. yellow cake mix

Cut 12 to 18 12-inch squares of heavy-duty foil; set aside. Cut 1-inch slice from top of each orange. Scoop out orange fruit and pulp. Leave peel intact as a baking cup. Prepare cake according to package directions. Fill each orange peel 2/3 full with prepared cake batter. Replace top of each orange. Place one filled orange in center of foil piece. Bring foil together at top and twist to make airtight. Place in coals for 15 to 20 minutes. Serves 12 to 18.

Banana Boat

A delicious dessert to cook in coals.

4 bananas, unpeeled
1/2 cup milk-chocolate pieces
1/2 cup miniature marshmallows

Cut a wedge-shaped section in each banana. Pull back peel. Remove wedge-shaped piece of banana. Fill cavity with milk-chocolate chips and marshmallows. Replace peeling over filling. Wrap securely in heavy-duty foil. Heat about 5 minutes over coals until chocolate and marshmallows melt. Serves 4.

Meatloaf In An Onion

An unusual family treat.

1 lb. lean ground beef
1 egg
1/4 cup cracker crumbs
1/4 cup tomato sauce
1/8 teaspoon pepper
1/2 teaspoon salt
1/2 teaspoon dry mustard
6 large onions, peeled

Cut six 12x14'' rectangles of heavy-duty foil; set aside. In a medium bowl, mix ground beef, egg, cracker crumbs, tomato sauce, pepper, salt and dry mustard. Set aside. Cut onions in half horizontally and remove centers, leaving 1/4-inch shell. Chop onion centers. Stir 2 tablespoons into meat mixture. Spoon meat mixture into 6 onion halves, rounding on top. Place remaining onion halves on top of filled onion halves. Place 1 filled onion on each piece of foil. Bring ends of foil up over onion. Fold foil down in small folds. Press sides of foil close to onion. Flatten ends and roll toward onion. Cook on coals 14 to 20 minutes on each side. Serves 6.

Tom studies Dian's holiday package-wrapping techniques.

Holidays

What's more exciting than preparing for a favorite holiday? These special days are marked by good food, good friends and good times. They're what memories are made of.

This chapter contains ideas for three major holidays: Thanksgiving, Christmas and New Year's Day. Suggestions for other holidays can be found in Chapter 5.

Here's a potpourri of food to eat and things to make for these special days. Some ideas will save you time and energy. Some will create new traditions for your family. Involve every member of the family and share in the joy of creating a truly memorable holiday!

TURKEY TIPS

1. To store a fresh turkey, loosely cover it with waxed paper or foil. Keep in the coldest part of your refrigerator and cook within 3 days.
2. Keep a frozen turkey in the freezer until you want to cook it. Whole turkeys can be kept frozen for one year; turkey parts for 6 months. After cooking, turkey may be stored 3 or 4 days in the refrigerator or frozen and stored up to 3 months.
3. Thaw your frozen turkey in the refrigerator, in cold water or at room temperature. Leave the plastic wrapper on. For even thawing at room temperature, place the wrapped turkey in a brown paper bag.
4. The refrigerator is the best place to thaw your turkey—it keeps meat cold while it defrosts. Allow 5 hours per pound to thaw.

THANKSGIVING HELPS

Everyone from football fans to food lovers looks forward to Thanksgiving. These suggestions will make Thanksgiving a feastlover's delight. For the kitchen crew behind the scenes, these helps are a delight, too.

HELPFUL TURKEY-DAY IDEAS
Chopped Onion Without Tears—Take the tears out of preparing onions by chopping them in your blender. Cut an onion in quarters or eighths. Fill blender half-full with water. Add onion pieces. Push chop button on and off until onion is chopped to desired size. Drain onions in a colander. Repeat until you have enough onions for your recipe.

Double-Stuff The Turkey—If guests or family members prefer different kinds of stuffing, double-stuff the turkey. Stuff neck cavity with one kind of dressing and tail/back cavity with a different kind. You might fill one cavity with celery stuffing and the other with oyster stuffing.

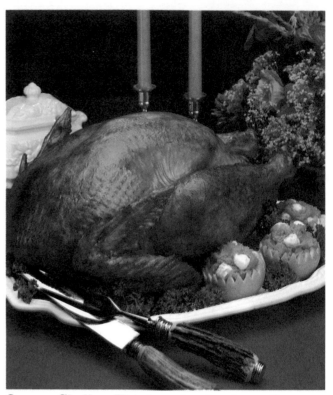

Unstuff The Turkey Instantly—Unstuffing the turkey is a cinch using this technique. The key is a cheesecloth bag put in the turkey to hold the stuffing.

To make bag, cut a piece of cheesecloth large enough to cover inside of turkey cavity with several inches extra. This will probably be a 20- to 25-inch square. Stitch cloth to form a two-sided bag. Tuck bag into turkey with unstitched edges poking out. Spoon dressing into bag until cavity is loosely filled. Fold bag closed and tuck edges up into cavity. Secure bag by folding drumsticks under wire holder or thick skin that holds legs together.

After turkey is cooked, open stuffing bag and spoon out a little dressing. Grasp outside edges of the bag firmly and pull out of turkey—dressing and all. No dressing will be left in turkey. Empty dressing into a dish and serve.

Orange Shells—This is a simple, decorative way to serve yams or sweet potatoes. Cut oranges in half and remove fruit and pulp. Add fruit to holiday punch. Prepare cooked yams or sweet potatoes and spoon into orange shells. Nestle oranges around turkey on the platter. For an extra touch, flute top edges of orange shell with a knife and top with maraschino cherry. Try the following recipe for delicious yams or sweet potatoes.

Yam-Stuffed Oranges

A new way to serve yams.

3 cups cooked, mashed yams or sweet potatoes
3 tablespoons butter or margarine
3 tablespoons orange juice
3/4 teaspoon salt
1 cup miniature marshmallows
3 tablespoons apricot jam
4 oranges

Heat yams or sweet potatoes. Stir in butter or margarine, orange juice, salt, marshmallows and jam. Preheat oven to 325F (165C). Cut oranges in half. Use a spoon to scoop out fruit and pulp. Spoon mixture into the orange shells. Arrange on baking sheet. Bake 15 to 20 minutes or until marshmallows melt and yams are hot. When turkey comes out of oven, yams go in. When turkey is ready to serve, yams will be hot. Makes 6 to 8 servings.

Turkey Carving Tips—Just out of the oven, with juices dripping, the turkey looks and smells wonderful. To graciously serve it from platter to plate, try these carving techniques.

1. Remove the drumstick and thigh by pressing leg away from body. Joint connecting leg to backbone may snap free. If it doesn't, use a sharp knife and cut leg from backbone. Cut dark meat completely from bone structure by following body contour carefully with a knife.

2. Cut drumsticks and thighs apart by cutting through joint. Place thighs on separate plate. It's easy to cut meat if you tilt drumstick to a convenient angle and slice toward plate.

3. To slice thigh meat, hold piece firmly on the plate with a fork. Cut even slices parallel to the bone.

4. Remove half the breast at a time by cutting along the breastbone and rib cage with a sharp knife. Lift meat away from the bone.

5. Place a half breast on a cutting surface and slice evenly against grain of the meat. Repeat with second half of the breast when additional slices are needed. End result is a beautifully carved turkey.

THANKSGIVING PLANOVERS

Festivities may end the day after Thanksgiving, but turkey and trimmings linger on and on. With these ideas for tasty turkey dishes, people will be asking for more. Try the following recipes to recycle Thanksgiving goodies.

Turkey Salad Sandwich

A tasty treat.

1/2 cup finely diced celery
2 cups diced cooked turkey
1/4 cup minced green onion
2 hard-cooked eggs, chopped
1 tablespoon lemon juice
1/2 teaspoon salt
3/4 cup mayonnaise
Dash red (cayenne) pepper

Combine all ingredients in a medium bowl, mixing well. Cover and refrigerate 3 to 4 hours to let flavors blend. Makes 3 cups sandwich filling.

Turkey Salad Olé

A great buffet!

Crisp tortilla shells or
**   taco-flavored tortilla chips**
Lettuce, shredded
Green onions, chopped
Refried beans
Cooked turkey, diced or shredded
Monterrey Jack cheese, coarsely grated
Avocado slices
Sour cream
Taco sauce

Prepare each ingredient according to the number of people you expect to serve. Place them in individual serving dishes. Cover with plastic wrap and refrigerate until ready to serve. At serving time, arrange ingredients and let everyone help themselves.

Turkey Divan

A tasty combination.

1 (10-oz.) pkg. frozen broccoli spears
6 to 8 slices leftover turkey
1 (10-1/2-oz.) can condensed Cheddar-
cheese soup
2 tablespoons milk
1/2 cup mayonnaise
1-1/2 teaspoons lemon juice
1/4 teaspoon curry powder
1 cup sliced almonds

Steam broccoli until tender but firm. Preheat oven to 350F (175C). Grease a 2-quart casserole dish. Arrange steamed broccoli over bottom of dish. Add a layer of sliced turkey. In a medium bowl, combine soup, milk, mayonnaise, lemon juice and curry powder. Pour over top of turkey. Sprinkle with sliced almonds. Heat casserole 15 to 20 minutes in a 350F (175C) oven. Serve with Onion Rice, if desired. Serves 4.

Leftover Dressing Mold—This easy dish uses uncooked dressing you have left over after Thanksgiving. Press dressing into heavily greased ring mold and place mold in large freezer bag. Freeze until needed.

Remove from freezer bag. Bake at 350F (175C) until mixture turns light golden brown, 45 minutes to 1 hour. Invert dressing onto a platter and serve with leftover turkey and gravy.

Onion Rice

A quick-and-easy dish.

2 cups prepared onion soup
1 cup rice

In a medium pan, bring soup to a boil over medium-high heat. Stir in rice. Cover pan. Turn heat to low. Continue to cook for 30 minutes. Serves 6.

Snow-White Turkey Salad

A delicious salad.

4 cups diced cooked turkey
1 cup thinly sliced celery
1 cup minced green pepper
1/4 cup finely chopped onion
1 cup mayonnaise
1/4 cup whipping cream, whipped
1 teaspoon chicken bouillon granules
1 teaspoon salt
1/8 teaspoon pepper
Lettuce, shredded
Garnishes of your choice

Combine turkey, celery, green pepper and onion in a bowl. Set aside. In another bowl combine mayonnaise, whipped cream, bouillon granules, salt and pepper. Mix well. Fold into turkey-vegetable mixture. Refrigerate until serving time. Mound turkey salad on crisp lettuce and circle with desired garnishes. Delicious garnishes might include toasted almonds, sliced apples, grapes, pineapple chunks, avocado slices or hard-cooked eggs. Serves 6 to 8.

Turkey Soup Stock

Make ahead to use when needed.

1 turkey carcass
4 to 5 qts. cold water
2 to 3 stalks celery
2 to 3 large onions, sliced
3 carrots
Salt and pepper

Place carcass in a large heavy pan. Cover with 4 to 5 quarts cold water. Add vegetables and seasonings. Bring to a boil. Cover and reduce heat. Simmer about 5 hours. Remove bones. Drain remaining broth through cheesecloth to strain out vegetables and small bones. Cool the broth in the refrigerator until fat solidifies. Skim off fat. Use broth for delicious soups or as a base for gravies or sauces. Freeze broth in ice-cube trays and bread pans, then pop out and store in freezer bags to use later. Makes 4 quarts of broth.

POTPOURRI OF CHRISTMAS IDEAS

"Christmas is coming, the goose is getting fat" goes the old carol. But as Christmas approaches, your wallet tends to get thinner and thinner. These inexpensive, yet novel, gifts and decorations will help make your Christmas merry without depleting your budget.

CREATE A MEMORABLE CHRISTMAS

It's not hard to make Christmas one of the most special days of the year. Use these ideas and tips to help make your Christmas the greatest.

Christmas Tree And Present Box — A great gift for friends or relatives who might not have a Christmas tree is to include a tree with the gifts.

Obtain a shoe box, dress box or coat box. If box has a separate lid, use a wide piece of tape to make a hinge so lid opens only one way. You may wish to wrap the top and bottom individually with Christmas wrapping before you hinge the top.

Cut a Christmas tree shape from green construction paper or draw a tree on paper. Make tree just large enough to fit into top of box and paste it inside of lid. Decorate the Christmas tree with little colored ornaments of paper. When box opens, tree stands upright with presents at its base.

Portrait Christmas Stockings — Make a portrait Christmas stocking for each member of the family. Sew or buy a large Christmas stocking for each person. Every year add a new school photo to the stocking.

Christmas Tree For The Birds — Use a small evergreen tree or gather four to six 12-inch branches from evergreen shrubs. Tie together in the center to look like a Christmas tree. Attach enough wire or cord to the top to tie the "tree" to a fence or tree branch outside. Decorate with stringed berries, bread cubes, marshmallows, popcorn, crackers, cereal or other items birds will eat. Sprinkle with bird seed. Share your Christmas with the birds as you watch them eat the goodies.

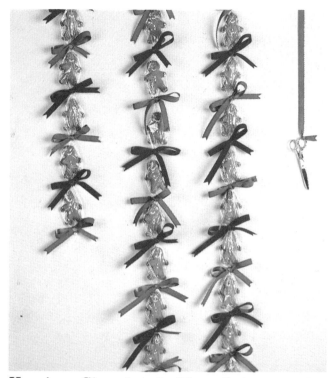

Hanging Gingerbread Men—String together some gingerbread men as a tasty farewell treat for visitors. To make the string, roll out 10 to 12 feet of plastic wrap. Place decorated gingerbread men face down lengthwise about 2 inches apart along the wrap. Fold wrap in from both sides, overlapping it to cover gingerbread men. Use colorful red and green Christmas ribbons to tie a secure bow around the wrap between each gingerbread man. Top the string with a large, full bow. Hang your colorful string of gingerbread men beside the front door. As holiday guests leave, snip off a gingerbread treat for them to munch on their way.

Pop-Can Carolers—Your children will enjoy making these ornaments as much as you will. Use aluminum soda cans with pop-top openings. Squeeze cans in the center with your hands. Lay the can on a sidewalk or concrete floor and step carefully on the center of it, smashing it into a compact can. Top of can should still be intact.

To decorate can, lay it top down on newspapers and paint with red or green enamel paint. When paint dries, turn can top-side up and paint the face with pink or flesh-colored enamel. Using pop-tab hole as the caroler's singing mouth, paint in eyes, nose and other features. You may wish to add small pompons on the corner of the can to signify a hat. To hang the ornament, punch a hole in the top rim of the can. Thread an 8- to 10-inch piece of yarn through the hole. Hang it on your tree.

Tin-Can Card Holder—Make your Christmas cards easy to read with this handy holder. Cut both ends from a tall, narrow can. Potato-chip cans work well. Secure red or green yarn to the inside of can with masking or filament tape. Wind yarn up and down inside and outside of can until yarn completely covers it. Strips of yarn should be close together. Secure end of yarn to inside of can with another piece of tape.

Slip Christmas card under one strip of yarn so yarn holds it to can along fold of card. Card hangs open and makes it easy to read special messages all through the holidays.

Wish Book—This special notebook will help everyone select gifts for other family members through the year. Prepare a medium-size notebook with a section for each person in the family. Each person's section includes a page for clothing sizes. Other pages list items needed and items wanted.

The notebook can be covered with fabric, wrapping paper or contact paper. When ideas for presents are needed, family members can glance at the book and select a perfect gift. Keep the notebook and use it year after year. Save the "wish lists" to share and enjoy as years pass.

Christmas Scrapbook—A wonderful Christmas tradition is to create your own family Christmas book. First find a large scrapbook or photo album. Then each year, place photos and a description of Christmas activities in the book. Save special letters, cards and other mementos of the holidays. Every year, add another section. Before

long, you'll have years of family Christmas memories to enjoy.

Jelly Thank-Yous

A nice way to say thank you.

2 (2-oz.) pkgs. pectin
1 (46-oz.) can apple drink or apple juice
7-1/2 cups sugar
1/2 teaspoon mint flavoring and
 1/2 teaspoon green food coloring or
1-1/2 teaspoons imitation berry flavoring and
 1/2 teaspoon red food coloring
Liquid paraffin

Stir pectin and apple drink or juice in heavy saucepan until smooth. Bring to a boil. Add sugar all at once. Continue stirring and bring to a rolling boil. Boil rapidly 2 minutes. Remove from heat and skim off foam. Add flavoring and coloring. Pour red or green jelly into sterilized decorative glasses. Seal with paraffin and tie with matching red or green ribbon. Makes 10 cups.

Christmas Tree In A Playpen—A Christmas tree is very attractive, especially to little ones. Try this idea—it could save your tree!

Put your decorated tree in a baby's playpen. Tree and packages will be safe and the little ones can still enjoy it. For a decorative touch, add a big bow to each corner of the playpen.

Snowman Centerpiece

This jolly snowman can be made in any size.

1/2 cup butter or margarine
1 (16-oz.) pkg. miniature marshmallows
1 teaspoon salt
20 cups popped popcorn
Black top hat
Candy for face and buttons

Melt butter or margarine in large saucepan over low heat. Add marshmallows and salt. Stir until completely melted. Continue stirring 3 minutes. Remove from heat. Pour over popped corn and stir until well coated.

While mixture is still warm, shape with buttered fingers into large ball, medium ball and small ball. To secure balls on top of one another, form small "bowl" in top of bottom ball and bump on bottom of middle ball. Do the same for two top balls. When balls are put together, bump fills bowl and holds balls in place.

Decorate with top hat, candy face and buttons.

Puffed-Rice Christmas Tree

A Christmas tree to delight anyone!

1/2 cup butter or margarine
1 (16-oz.) pkg. miniature marshmallows
6 cups puffed rice cereal
2 teaspoons green food coloring
1 cup cinnamon candies
1/2 cup silver cake decorating candies

Melt butter or margarine over low heat in large saucepan. Add marshmallows and food coloring. Stir until marshmallows are completely melted. Add rice cereal. While mixture is warm, form small balls with buttered fingers. Place several balls in a circle. Layer balls on top of each other in smaller circles to form Christmas-tree shape. Add extra filling between balls to give tree softer look. Decorate with cinnamon and silver candies.

CHRISTMAS MEMORY-MAKERS

Traditions and Christmas—they're a real duet and what special music they make. Adapt the best of these ideas for your family traditions.

Grandparents' Taped Stories—A personalized storybook is a wonderful gift for grandparents to give young children. Buy a storybook and record it on a blank cassette tape. Each time you turn a page, pause long enough to rap a glass tumbler with a spoon or ring a bell. The ding tells the child to turn the page. The recorded cassette-book will provide hours of pleasure and memories of a loving grandparent.

A personal book will be even more meaningful to your grandchild. Use photos, mementos and your own words to create a fiction story or an autobiography. Buy a book with blank pages or make your own from material, cardboard and glue. When book is finished, read it on a tape for a priceless treasure.

Holiday Planning Calendar—Planning makes perfect during the holidays. At the beginning of the Christmas season, family members get together and list Christmas activities on a large appointment or desk-blotter-size calendar. Shopping trips with smaller children, parties, Christmas concerts, the day for tree selection and trimming, even Christmas-wrapping and cookie-baking sessions are written on the calendar. Being able to see the holiday season at a glance will help coordinate family plans.

Family Christmas Book—Here's a gift of personal expression that's ideal for Chrismas Eve. Put the name of each family member on the top of a separate sheet of paper. On each sheet, have each family member write down one good memory of that person during the past year. The written memory might be an experience shared, a kindness done, a good attribute noticed or an amusing anecdote. Papers can be preserved in scrapbooks or memory boxes for rereading later.

Mr. and Mrs. Santa Brooms—This is a clever idea for Christmas. You'll need:

Santa

1 6" Styrofoam ball
1 piece 24 x 14" short red fur
6 1" white pompons (for hat)
1   2/3" red pompon (nose)
1 piece 24 x 5" short white fur (hatband)
1 piece 12 x 12" long white fur (beard)
1 piece 24 x 6" long white fur (hair)
2 eyes
Straight pins
Pink spray paint
1 broom

Mrs. Santa

1 6" Styrofoam ball
2 pieces 12 x 12" short red fur (dress and cap)
1 16" piece of 1/4-inch elastic (cap)
1 3/4" red pompon (nose)
1 piece 14 x 4" short white fur (shawl)
1 piece 24 x 8" long white fur (hair)
3 yards white lace
Buttons (red)
2 black pipe cleaners (for glasses)
1 red pipe cleaner (mouth)
2 eyes
Straight pins
Glue
1 broom

Drill holes through Styrofoam balls with a long wood bit. Make hole 1/8" smaller than diameter of broom handle for a tight fit. (A long thin-bladed knife could also be used to cut hole.)

Spray each ball pink and let dry. Place one ball on each broom handle. Glue eyes in place on balls. Glue on noses. Set aside until dry. Make glasses with pipe cleaners about 1/2" longer to press into the ball to hold in place.

Shape beard and glue in place using straight pins to hold until glue dries. Use straight pins without glue if you don't want a permanent bond. Put hair in place and fasten. Brush Mrs. Santa's hair up and form curls as desired. Brush Santa's hair down.

Using the short red fur, make a cone hat. Sew and place seam in back. Trim with short white fur and white pompons.

Using straw-end of the broom as a pattern, shape dress and measure to length. Trim with lace, buttons and ribbon. Place shawl around shoulders and pin in place.

Family Portrait Ornaments—Add a very special ornament to the family Christmas tree each year. Have a family Christmas photograph taken annually. Make it into a Christmas tree ornament. You'll create a wonderful tradition as well as a photo history of your family. Each ornament will be a valuable treasure as years pass and your family grows.

JOLLY CHRISTMAS WRAP

Look at common household discards such as newspapers, cardboard boxes, advertising circulars and paper bags. Can you see them as colorful wraps for Christmas gifts? With a little innovation, they can make your presents distinctive.

Unused Fabric—Use leftover fabric as gift wrap.

Newspapers—Plain newsprint or newspapers topped with a red or black bow can make attractive and inexpensive wrapping for large, hard-to-cover gifts. Newspapers also work well when you run short of holiday wrapping and need an emergency coverup. For more colorful packaging, use the comic section or advertising flyers and a matching or contrasting bow.

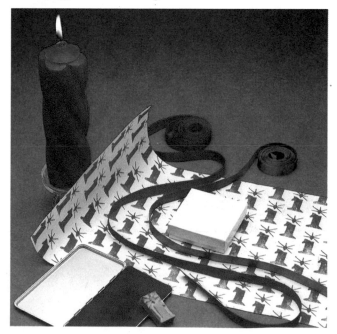

Along with ribbons and bows, use candy canes, all-day suckers, small plush toys, Christmas corsages, outdated or unused Christmas tree ornaments, holly or other seasonal substitutes to decorate your packages.

Gum-Eraser Print Wrap—To give children something to do besides present-peeping, have them make their own wrap. Purchase a large 1x2" gum eraser. Carve a design about 1/4 inch into eraser. Ink eraser on a stamp pad or with poster paint. Press a design on plain newsprint or other paper suitable for wrapping. For larger designs, use the same method with a potato. Cut it in half and carve your design on the flat side.

Shopping Bags—Many stores provide seasonal or unusual shopping bags for customers, particularly at Christmastime. These bags make great wrap for oddly shaped gifts. Staple the bag closed, then top with a bright bow. Bag may also be used as wrapping paper.

Brown Bag—With white typewriter correction fluid, make polka-dot brown paper gift wrap. If you're wrapping a box, wrap bottom in plain brown paper and lid in polka-dot paper.

Wallpaper Wrap—Check out odds and ends of wallpaper you may have. Wrap gifts with these scraps. Your choice can follow a color scheme.

A Box In A Box In A Box—Surprise the recipient of a small gift (jewelry, money, trinkets) by placing the present in a tiny box. Put the tiny box in a slightly larger box, then a larger one, and so on. You can wrap each box individually before placing it in the larger container. If you're giving a car, washing machine or gift that can't be boxed, put a note in last graduated box with directions leading to the hidden gift. The ensuing treasure hunt will be almost as much fun as the present.

Travel Poster And Road Map—Wrap gift in an old road map or poster.

Knee-Socks With Shoelaces—Wrap your present in a present. Place small gifts or fruit inside knee socks. Use shoelaces to tie bow between each gift.

Copy Machine Photo Wrap—Lay several photos on a copy machine. Leave 1/4 inch between them. Copy. If you need a large sheet of paper, tape several copies together.

Paper Tablecloth Wrap—Wrap large gifts in a paper Christmas tablecloth. A plain white paper cloth with a red bow and holly sprig is very attractive.

JANUARY

S	M	T	W	T	F	S
				1	2	3	4
5	6	7	8	9	10	11
12	13	14	15	16	17	18
19	20	21	22	23	24	25
26	27	28	29	30	31	

NEW YEAR'S DAY

Casual activities and light food are perfect for New Year's Day. Here are a few easy, tasty ways to keep your day relaxed.

Touchdown Munch

Great to munch while watching football New Year's Day.

2 tablespoons butter or margarine
1/4 cup honey
1 tablespoon lemon peel, grated
1/4 teaspoon cinnamon
2 quarts popcorn, popped
1-1/2 cups golden raisins
1-1/2 cups dried apricots, diced
1-1/2 cups dry roasted peanuts

In small saucepan, melt butter or margarine. Stir in honey, lemon peel and cinnamon. Drizzle over popcorn in large bowl. Add raisins, apricots and peanuts. Toss gently until well mixed. Serve immediately or place individual portions in self-sealing storage bags. Makes 2-1/2 quarts.

Cheese Straws

Tasty treats.

1 lb. grated sharp Cheddar cheese
3/4 cup margarine*
2 cups all-purpose flour
1-1/4 teaspoons baking powder
1/2 teaspoon salt
3 drops Tabasco sauce
Dash red (cayenne) pepper or to taste

Have grated cheese and margarine at room temperature before starting. Sift flour with baking powder and salt. With hands, mix margarine and cheese well. Add Tabasco, red pepper and flour to margarine and cheese. Mix well and chill. Roll dough with hands into 2- to 3-inch sticks on lightly floured surface. Press on ungreased baking sheets.

Bake in preheated 300F (150C) oven 10 minutes. Reduce heat to 225F (105C) and bake 5 to 20 minutes longer until crisp. If you think straws are cooking too fast, leave oven door open. Makes about 100. These freeze well.

*Butter can be used, but straws will not keep as well. They will be more brittle and slightly greasy.

Cranberry Ice

Goes great with everything.

1 (12-oz.) pkg. fresh cranberries
2 cups sugar
1 qt. cold water
Juice of 3 lemons
1 teaspoon grated orange peel

In a saucepan, boil together cranberries, sugar and 2 cups cold water until berries pop. Process in blender until smooth. Add lemon juice, 2 cups cold water and orange peel. Freeze in container. Remove from freezer about 1 hour before serving. This very refreshing, light slush makes 10 cups.

Cranberry Ice and Cheese Straws.

IDEAS FOR A GREAT NEW YEAR'S

Take it easy New Year's morning. Watch television with an easy-to-make breakfast of German Oven Pancakes and Icy Fruit Whip.

Icy Fruit Whip

Tastes cool and refreshing.

1 banana
1 cup pineapple, fresh or canned
1 orange
5 to 10 ice cubes

In blender, process ingredients to an icy slush. Serve immediately. Makes 2 servings.

Hot Grape Punch

The whole family will love it.

6 cups water
1 qt. unsweetened grape juice
1 cup sugar
1 (6-oz.) can frozen lemonade concentrate
1 (6-oz.) can frozen orange-juice concentrate
Fruit slices

Mix ingredients in a large saucepan. Heat until warm. Serve in mugs. Makes 2-1/2 quarts.

German Oven Pancakes

A delicious way to celebrate the New Year.

1/2 cup milk
1/2 cup all-purpose flour
3 large eggs
Dash salt
2 tablespoons butter or margarine
1 (8-oz.) box frozen raspberries
1 (20-oz.) can of chunk pineapple, drained
4 bananas
1/2 cup firmly packed brown sugar
1 (8-oz.) container dairy sour cream

Put milk, flour, eggs and salt into mixing bowl and mix with fork or wire whip. Melt 1 tablespoon butter or margarine in each of two 9-inch pie plates in a preheated oven at 400F (205C). Butter should be sizzling. Swish butter around plate to grease bottom. Increase oven temperature to 425F (220C). Pour batter into pie plate until 1/4-inch thick. Bake 10 to 15 minutes or until golden brown. Edges will puff up. Pancake will form a well in the center. Spoon raspberries, pineapple and bananas into center of pancake. Sprinkle with brown sugar and top with sour cream. Serves 4.

New Year's Day Refreshers—You'll probably want light snacks to eat on New Year's Day while you watch football games, serve friends who drop in to say hello or read a good book.

It's a good idea to serve nutritious snacks. Try some of these.

- Hot cider.
- Cheese slices and crackers.
- Bread sticks.
- Sliced crisp vegetables with blue cheese salad dressing or cottage cheese blended smooth.
- Dried fruit with nuts, wheat nuts, sunflower seeds and coconut flakes.
- Deviled, hard-cooked eggs.
- Granola to snack on.
- Tomato juice with dash of onion salt and lemon juice, served with stick of celery.
- Celery with peanut butter and raisins or nuts.

Make-Ahead Dainties

These taste good any time.

1 lb. butter (not margarine)
1-1/2 cups granulated sugar
1-1/2 cups brown sugar
1/2 cup boiling water
3 eggs
2 teaspoons vanilla extract
6-1/2 cups all-purpose flour
1 teaspoon baking soda
1 teaspoon salt
1 lb. chopped walnuts
Red and green sugar decorations

In a large bowl, stir butter, sugars and water until smooth. Add eggs and mix thoroughly. Stir in vanilla. Sift flour, baking soda and salt together. Stir into egg mixture slowly. Add walnuts. Divide dough into 4 balls. Form each ball into a cylinder with a diameter the size of a half-dollar. Wrap each cylinder in plastic wrap and store in refrigerator. Dough can be stored 2 weeks in refrigerator and up to 6 months in freezer.

When you need a dessert in a hurry, slice off the number of cookies required. Be sure to slice them thin. Bake in preheated 350F (175C) oven 6 to 10 minutes, watching to make sure cookies do not brown. When edges begin to brown, they are done. To decorate, sprinkle hot cookies with colored sugar decoration. Cookies are especially tasty with mint ice cream, eggnog or your favorite punch. Makes 48 cookies.

Cereal Snack

Snack on this all day long.

1/3 cup butter or margarine
4 teaspoons Worcestershire sauce
1 teaspoon seasoning salt
6 cups wheat, corn or rice cereal
3/4 cup salted nuts
1 cup pretzels

Preheat oven to 250F (120C). In large saucepan melt butter or margarinc. Stir in Worcestershire sauce and salt. Add cereal, nuts and pretzels. Stir until all pieces are coated. Spread in jelly-roll pan. Heat in oven 30 to 45 minutes. Stir every 15 minutes until heated. Scrape onto a paper towel and blot until dry. Serve immediately or put in tightly covered containers for gifts or storage. Makes 6 cups.

Dian and Jane prepare treats for Halloween.

Special Days 5

All through the year there are special days for the entire family to share and enjoy. These are holidays, fun days and days of remembrance. Each has its own traditions.

This chapter provides you with many ideas for celebrations during the year. Halloween ideas are a treat to create. The variety of Valentine goodies will make it a special day. Sections on Easter and the 4th of July offer interesting food treats and wonderful ways to celebrate. Take your pick of these ideas and establish your own family traditions.

HALLOWEEN

Cheery witches, magic princesses, even scary monsters expect scrumptious treats and delightful tricks on Halloween. You'll please all the ghosts and goblins with these Halloween treats.

Apple Cider In A Jack-O-Lantern—This jack-o-lantern is a punchbowl and centerpiece. Thoroughly clean inside of pumpkin. Make sure you remove all the fibrous strings. Paint a jack-o-lantern face on pumpkin using acrylic paints or permanent marking pens. Refrigerate pumpkin until ready to serve the drink. Pour cider or other Halloween punch into cold pumpkin. Pumpkin cools your drink and delights your guests.

Dinner In A Pumpkin

A treat for the whole family.

1 small to medium pumpkin
1 onion, chopped
2 tablespoons vegetable oil
1-1/2 to 2 lbs. ground beef
2 tablespoons soy sauce
2 tablespoons brown sugar
1 (4-oz.) can sliced mushrooms, drained
1 (10-3/4-oz.) can cream-of-chicken soup
1-1/2 cups cooked rice
1 (8-oz.) can sliced water chestnuts, drained

Cut off the top of pumpkin and thoroughly clean out seeds and pulp. Paint an appropriate face on the front of the pumpkin with a permanent marking pen or acrylic paint. Preheat oven to 350F (175C). In a large skillet, sauté onions in oil until tender. Add meat and brown. Drain drippings from skillet. Add soy sauce, brown sugar, mushrooms and soup. Simmer 10 minutes, stirring occasionally. Add cooked rice and water chestnuts. Spoon mixture into the cleaned pumpkin shell. Replace pumpkin top and place entire pumpkin, with filling, on a baking sheet. Bake 1 hour or until inside meat of the pumpkin is tender. Put pumpkin on a plate. Remove pumpkin lid and serve meat. For your vegetable, scoop out cooked pumpkin and serve. Serves 6.

Dry-Ice Jack-O-Lantern—Create a spooky atmosphere with this eerie, steaming jack-o-lantern. Choose a pumpkin large enough to hold a No. 10 can (holds a little under a gallon). Clean pumpkin and carve a spooky face. Fill can about 3/4 full of hot water, 1/2 cup salt and mix. Place container in the pumpkin.

If there is room, place a flashlight or weather light between the pumpkin and container to add to the effect. Wear gloves to protect your hands. Drop two or three large pieces of dry ice into the container of water. Dry ice will steam up and out of the face of the pumpkin.

As water cools, ice will form around the dry ice, causing it to stop bubbling. Salt water will cause action to last longer. After 15 to 20 minutes, drain cold water from the container and replace it with hot water to start the reaction again.

Notched Jack-O-Lantern—To line up pumpkin lid more easily, cut a triangular notch on one side of pumpkin lid. It's easy to match the notch to replace the lid.

Coupon For Special Treaters—Give special witches and superheroes a gift coupon for a meal or treat at a local fast-food restaurant. A coupon for free fries, an ice-cream cone or other food treats can extend the Halloween fun for weeks after the holiday has ended.

Bundt Cake Jack-O-Lantern—Two Bundt cakes make an attractive jack-o-lantern. Use 3 cake mixes for this treat. Mix cake mixes according to package directions. Grease and flour pans well so cakes come out easily. Bake half the batter (1-1/2 cake mixes) in each of 2 large Bundt pans.

When cakes are done, remove from pans and cool. Cut rounded, raised top part from each cake to make it flat. Place one cake, narrow-side down, on plate. Matching ribs, lay other cake, wide-side down on top of first cake to form jack-o-lantern. Pipe on orange-frosting features. Stuff center hole with plastic wrap to just below the top.

To make a green stem and leaves for the top, blend 3 ounces cream cheese, at room temperature, with 3 cups powdered sugar. Stir cream cheese and slowly add sugar while whipping. Add few drops of green food coloring. Mold into stem and leaf shapes. Set into top of cake.

Orange Jack-O-Lanterns—Oranges can provide a nutritious snack for children. A fun project is to decorate oranges for trick-or-treaters or Halloween party favors. Make them into jack-o-lanterns by decorating with a permanent marker.

Starched Spooky Ghosts—You can see through ghosts if you make these spooky creatures. You'll need medium-size soda bottles, a large roll of bandage gauze, 2-inch Styrofoam balls and concentrated liquid starch. Put a Styrofoam ball in mouth of bottle. Cut strips of gauze long enough to drape over bottle. Saturate strips in undiluted starch solution. Drape gauze over soda bottle. Tie a white ribbon around the neck. Dry until stiff. When dry, separate bottle and Styrofoam ball. Add eyes to ghosts' heads. Ghosts will stand by themselves as table decorations.

Black Cat Doughnut Server—Doughnuts and cider aren't new for Halloween, but this cat server will make an old standby novel and fresh. Make it out of 3/4-inch plywood and a 3-foot dowel. Cut the cat's body and base out of plywood according to the pattern. Attach dowel tail to the plywood and paint black. Stack doughnuts on tail.

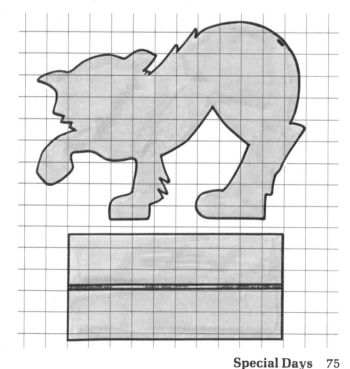

Ghost Sticks

Kids love these spooky treats!

3 lbs. white chocolate
Aluminum foil
Oil for greasing foil
15 to 20 wooden ice-cream sticks
42 chocolate pieces

Grate and melt white chocolate until smooth in top of double boiler over simmering water. Cover baking sheet with foil and grease lightly. Place sticks on baking sheet, 4 inches apart. Spoon melted white chocolate in ghost shapes over top of sticks. Use chocolate pieces for eyes. Refrigerate on baking sheets until chocolate is firm. Ghosts are tasty fund-raisers for school or church. Makes 15 to 20 ghosts.

Graveyard Cake—Make a haunting treat for your little ones. Use Fig Newtons or other flat cookies on a frosted sheet cake to form graves and headstones. Lay 2 cookies flat on cake to make grave. At head of each "cookie grave," set another cookie vertically to form headstone. You may decorate each headstone if you desire. Makes 1 cake.

Cemetery Scene—Combine white chocolate Ghost Sticks with Graveyard Cake for marvelously spookie effect. See photo above.

Roasted Pumpkin Seeds

Tastes best if you boil seeds first in salted water.

2 cups pumpkin seeds
1 teaspoon Worcestershire sauce
3 tablespoons butter or margarine, melted
1 teaspoon salt

Rinse pumpkin seeds until pulp and strings are washed off. Boil seeds in salt water for 10 minutes. Dry seeds on paper towel.

In medium bowl, combine Worcestershire sauce, melted butter or margarine and salt. Add seeds. Stir until seeds are coated with mixture. Spread on baking sheet. Bake 1 to 2 hours at 225F (105C). Stir occasionally and watch for burning. Seeds should be crisp. Makes 2 cups.

Ghost Suckers—For a creative treat to give neighborhood ghosts and goblins, make ghost-like suckers from string licorice, round suckers and soft white tissues. Place a sheet of tissue over the top of each sucker, gather it under candy and tie tissue with black string licorice. Make two dot eyes on your ghost with marker.

Halloween Sandwich Surprise—Make Halloween face on a cheese sandwich. Cut a jack-o-lantern face on one slice of bread. Add cheese and second slice of bread underneath bread face. Serve plain or toast under broiler. A clever combination is dark rye bread with yellow cheese.

Flash-O-Lanterns—Trick-or-treaters can have fun and be safe with flash-o-lanterns. You will need tissue paper, starch, a balloon and paint.

Blow up balloon and use it as a base to build a tissue head. Dip strips of tissue paper in liquid starch. Smooth onto balloon until balloon is completely covered. After each layer of tissue paper dries, add another layer. Repeat this process until balloon is covered with five to six layers of papier-maché.

When paper is completely dry, draw a face on the balloon. Cut out eyes, nose and mouth with a razor blade or knife. If balloon hasn't popped, pop it and pull it from inside the paper head. Now comes the fun. Let your trick-or-treaters decorate and paint the head. Use yarn or fake fur for hair.

Make a dot on center of the bottom. Draw a circle around dot using the end of the flashlight as a pattern. With a knife or razor blade, cut from the dot out to the drawn circle forming 6 to 8 wedges. Fold wedges to outside and insert flashlight. Tape wedges to flashlight with masking tape to hold head on. Tie ribbon around flashlight covering the taped wedges. Turn on flashlight and balloon head lights up!

Ghost Cake—This great cake will light up your celebration! Bake a sheet cake and frost with chocolate frosting. Make a ghost shape on the cake with white frosting. Use the stencil method on page 35. Fill in with more white frosting. Outline ghost shape with black rope licorice.

Place 2 empty eggshell halves where ghost's eyes would be. Place a sugar cube soaked in lemon extract in each shell. When ready to serve, light sugar cubes, turn off lights and watch your "flaming ghost."

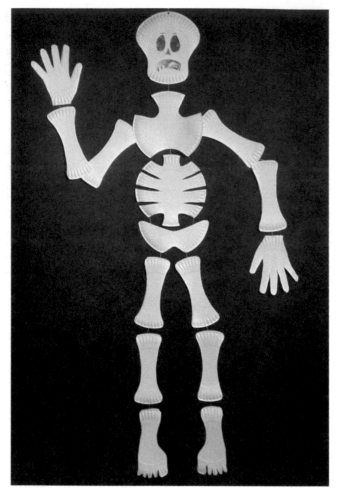

Paper-Plate Skeleton—Perfect for hanging from doors and windows, this scary skeleton is easy to make. Cut white paper plates according to pattern. Join parts of skeleton by punching small holes with paper punch at each point of contact. Tie parts together with string. Draw or paint features on skeleton's face. Accent skeleton's scary face by cutting out eyes, nose and mouth. Paste a sheet of black construction paper on back of plate so paper shows through holes. If both sides of skeleton will show, attach an additional paper plate to form back of head.

Ghost Chocolate Pie—Add an eerie Halloween decoration to your favorite chocolate pie. Pipe whipped topping in the form of a ghost on top of the pie. Use whipped topping in a pressurized can or put regular whipped topping in a decorator bag. Fill in the outline with more whipped topping. Add 2 chocolate pieces for eyes.

Shadow Shapes—This unusual jack-o-lantern showers the room with geometric lights. Cut three rows of triangles, circles or squares horizontally around a hollowed-out pumpkin. In a darkened room, candle inside pumpkin casts eerie, geometric shadows.

PAPER PLATE SKELETON

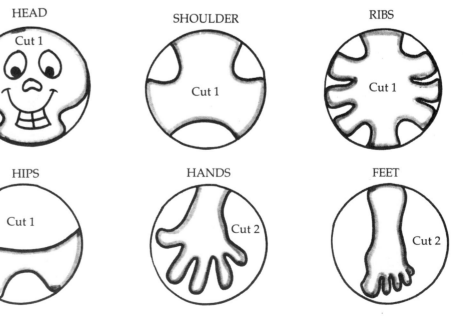

HEAD
Cut 1

SHOULDER
Cut 1

RIBS
Cut 1

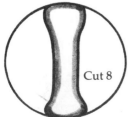

UPPER AND LOWER ARMS AND LEGS
Cut 8

HIPS
Cut 1

HANDS
Cut 2

FEET
Cut 2

S M T W T F S
                1
2 3 4 5 6 7 8
9 10 11 12 13 14 15
16 17 18 19 20 21 22
23 24 25 26 27 28

VALENTINE VARIETY

Valentine's Day presents the perfect opportunity for lighthearted expressions of love or friendship. Whether the object of your affection is a child of 2 or a grandparent of 82, he or she will enjoy one of these thoughtful Valentines.

Candy-Message Valentines—Give your friends a candy-bar hello. On a piece of posterboard, write your Valentine greeting so candy bar forms part of the message. Some suggested messages might include:

"I (mint) to ask you to be my Valentine."

"Valentine, you stole a (Big Hunk) of my heart."

"I chews (gum) you to be my Valentine."

"You're the (Cup o' Gold) at the end of my rainbow."

"I'd run a (Marathon bar) for you, Valentine."

Heart-Shape Cupcakes—Heart-shape cupcakes are easy to make. Use your favorite cupcake recipe. Place paper baking cups in a muffin-tin. Put a marble or small ball of foil in each cup between paper liner and pan. This makes heart-shape mold in which to cook cupcakes. Pour in cake batter and bake as usual. Don't fill cups too full or you will lose the heart-shape effect of the cupcake.

Sweet Valentine Bouquet—To make a bouquet for a gift or centerpiece, use a clean flowerpot or empty can. Paint can or flowerpot red or cover with Valentine's Day wrapping paper. Glue eyelet lace around top and bottom of can. Purchase 2 dozen flower-shaped cookies with holes in the center, 1 to 2 dozen large heart-shaped red gumdrops, 1 to 2 dozen bamboo skewers and 2 3-inch-thick pieces of Styrofoam to fit in can.

Glue Styrofoam to inside bottom of can. To make flowers, push a skewer through center of one of the gumdrops, through center of a cookie and then another gumdrop. Push cookie and gumdrops together sandwich-style on end of skewer. Insert other end of skewer into Styrofoam inside flowerpot. Tie a red bow under the cookie.

Cut skewers so flowers will be different heights. Add green asparagus fern, available from a florist, to contrast with your bouquet. Idea can be used all year by substituting colored gumdrops for heart-shaped gumdrops and changing the color of ribbon.

Super Kiss

Give someone special a super kiss.

1/4 cup margarine or butter
1 (10-oz.) pkg. marshmallows (about 50) or
**   4 cups miniature marshmallows**
5 cups rice cereal or chocolate rice cereal

Melt margarine or butter in large saucepan over low heat. Add marshmallows and stir until completely melted. Stirring constantly, cook 3 minutes longer over low heat. Remove from heat. Add cereal and stir until well-coated. Cool slightly but not completely. Butter your fingers. Press warm mixture into large, buttered funnels. When cool, unmold from funnel and wrap in plastic. Makes 2 to 4 large kisses.

Photo-Valentine—Give grandparents a special valentine. Have children decorate a red construction-paper heart. Cut out a heart-shape from the middle of the valentine. Glue child's school picture or other recent picture in the heart shape. If children make one each year, grandparents will have a collection of special valentines to save over the years.

Heart-Shape Edibles—Give a heart February 14th by serving heart-shape biscuits and gelatin. If you don't have a deep, heart-shape cookie cutter make one from a tuna can. Cut both ends from can and wash can thoroughly. Mold can into heart-shape by pressing in on each edge opposite the seam. Cut biscuit dough and gelled gelatin with heart-shape cutter. Slip servings onto platter or serving dishes with pancake turner.

Valentine Dessert

This delicate dessert will capture anyone's heart.

4 egg whites
1/4 teaspoon cream of tartar
Dash of salt
1 cup sugar
1 teaspoon vanilla extract
Few drops of red food coloring, optional
1 qt. strawberry ice cream
1 (8-oz.) jar strawberry topping

Beat egg whites, cream of tartar and salt until stiff but not dry. Add sugar, 1 tablespoon at a time, beating until stiff after each addition. Fold in vanilla and add food coloring, if desired. Cover baking sheet with heavy, brown grocery bag. Spoon meringue in heart shapes onto baking sheet. Make a depression in the center. Bake in 250F (120C) oven 40 to 60 minutes or until lightly browned. Remove at once from paper. Fill shell with strawberry ice cream and top with topping. Serves 2.

Heart Cake Without A Special Pan—Make a heart cake without purchasing a special pan. You'll need a 9-inch round cake pan and a 9-inch square baking pan. Pour cake batter in pans and bake. Cool cake and remove from pans. Place square cake diamond-fashion on large platter or dish you're going to decorate the cake on. Cut round cake in half. Place each half with cut side next to the square side. You may need to trim corners. This creates a large heart. Frost with white frosting and make border around top. Fill with cherry pie-filling.

To keep cake from rising higher in middle while baking, place wet paper towels in narrow strips around outside edge of cake pan. Outside edge will cook slower, making cake flat. See photograph.

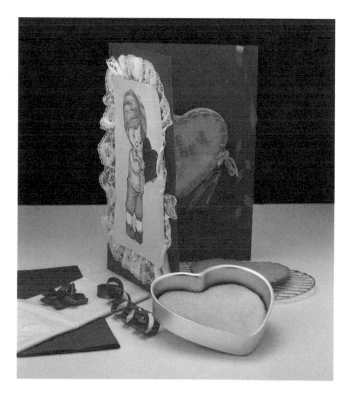

Giant Cookie Heart—Be big-hearted on Valentine's Day and make an oversize cookie heart. Make a large heart-shape paper pattern or use a heart-shape cake pan. You will also need prepared sugar-cookie mix.

Grease a baking sheet. Roll out dough on counter. Use heart-shape pan or pattern as a cookie cutter. Cut out cookie. Lift giant cookie by placing a rolling pin at the top of the cookie. Carefully lift dough onto rolling pin and roll cookie toward you around rolling pin. Unroll it onto baking sheet. Bake at 375F (190C) 10 to 12 minutes. Cool and remove. Frost and decorate as desired.

PRESIDENTS' DAY

Take time to make a special dish in honor of George Washington and Abraham Lincoln.

Old Glory Cake

A glorious cake to see!

1 9x13'' sheet cake, frosted white
1 (21-oz.) can blueberry pie-filling
1 (21-oz.) can cherry pie-filling or
**   2 qts. fresh strawberries, sliced**

Create the first American flag on your white-frosted sheet cake. See accompanying photo for guide to making flag. Spread blueberry pie-filling over a rectangle in one corner. Dot 13 white-icing stars in a circle on blue background. Arrange cherry pie-filling or strawberry slices across remainder of cake to form stripes. Fill in borders and white stripes with frosting. Makes 1 sheet cake.

Lincoln-Log Cake—Bake your family's favorite chocolate-cake recipe in a 46-ounce juice can. Remove 1 end. Grease, cut and fit a circular piece of waxed paper in bottom of can. Fill 2/3 full with cake batter. Stand 2 straws vertically in cake batter. Pour remaining batter around straws, filling can 3/4 full. Plastic straws can be used if cut off 1 to 2 inches above batter. Straws allow air to be released from bottom of pan so cake will rise properly.

Bake cake until you can lift a straw without batter sticking to it. Allow cake to cool. With can opener, remove bottom of can and slide cake out. Place cool cake on a plate and decorate with favorite light-chocolate frosting.

You can make a frosting bag by cutting out a corner from a heavy plastic bag. Fill bag with darker chocolate frosting. Clip end and begin decorating by going horizontally back and forth across the cake. On both ends, use darker frosting to create rings. Top frosted cake with 3 stemmed maraschino cherries and place a miniature paper hatchet into the log. Use pattern at left.

Washington's Cherry Tarts—You won't be telling a lie when you say these tarts are delicious. Using a standard pie-crust recipe, make cherry-tart crusts in small foil pans. Prick them with a fork. Cut out pie-crust hatchets using pattern drawn on heavy paper. Bake crusts and hatchets. Fill crusts with cherry pie-filling and place a hatchet on top of each tart.

ST. PATRICK'S DAY

An unusual way to celebrate St. Patrick's Day is to serve green food. Stuffed green peppers, green salad, green beans or peas, lime gelatin salad or lime punch all fill the bill. Add to your menu a luscious Green Fruit Chill or Lime-Chocolate Smoothie.

Lime-Chocolate Smoothies

A lively dessert for St. Paddy's Day.

1 (3-oz.) pkg. lime gelatin
1 (8-oz.) container whipped topping
1 cup chopped nuts
1/2 cup chocolate pieces
1/2 cup cookie crumbs or toasted coconut

Prepare gelatin with water as directed on package. Use ice cubes to hasten thickening. When thickened, remove ice cubes and add 1 cup of whipped topping. Beat until smooth. Blend in remaining whipped topping. Stir in nuts and chocolate pieces. Refrigerate 15 minutes. Serve in a dish sprinkled with cookie crumbs or toasted coconut. Or when firm enough, roll into balls and roll balls in cookie or coconut mixture. Makes 16 to 20 balls.

Green Fruit Chill

A tempting treat to eat.

4 cups bite-size pear chunks or pear halves, chilled
1 cup sweet liquid tinted with green food coloring (pineapple juice, limeade, carbonated lime)
1 qt. lime sherbet
6 green maraschino cherries
6 green mint leaves

Mix fruit with liquid and chill thoroughly. Before serving, spoon fruit mixture into sherbet or parfait glasses. Top with scoop of sherbet, maraschino cherry and mint-leaf garnish. Serves 6.

EGG-CITING EASTER IDEAS

You'd have to be egg-centric not to associate colored eggs with Easter. The following tips and ideas can help you make great-tasting possibilities for Easter.

Easter Treasure Hunt—Make your messages extra fun by including them as part of a treasure hunt. Hide the egg containing a clue in your child's Easter basket. If you don't want to blow out the egg, write the clue in fine-tipped marking pen on the outside of the egg. You may want to send your child on his Easter treasure hunt with a message such as, "A surprise is waiting under the kitchen table."

Another egg hunt makes finding eggs fun for children of all ages. Assign a particular color to each child. Hide colored eggs. Because an older child will hunt only for his color eggs, hide them in less obvious places than eggs hidden for younger children.

"I Love You" Eggs—Personalize your eggs by enclosing Easter messages in the shells. Blow out raw eggs and enclose message. Use a sharp needle to poke a small hole in the small end of each egg and a larger hole in big end. Through the larger hole, puncture the egg yolk with the needle. Hold egg over a bowl and gently blow through the small hole to force the raw egg out of the large hole. Rinse shells thoroughly but carefully.

Decorate blown-out eggshells with marking pen, ribbon, lace or watercolor paints. Write messages on small slips of paper. Roll up and carefully and place inside eggs through the larger hole.

King Or Queen Egg Hunt—Turn a traditional Easter-egg hunt into a real party by giving an extra treat to the finders of specially decorated eggs. For example, decorate a king egg and a queen egg or paint one egg gold and one silver. Hide them well so finders earn their treats.

Easter Bread-Basket—Use a loaf of bread before it is sliced. Cut top off bread, leaving sides and a handle of a basket. Hollow out bread so Easter goodies can be placed inside. Trim with ribbon. Grind unused bread for bread crumbs. See photograph.

Hairy Egghead Garden—Not all eggs must be bald. With your help they won't be hairless eggheads. Gently crack off the top quarter of a raw egg. Rinse eggshell well, leaving a hollow shell head. Using marking pens or paint, draw a face on the shell, omitting hair. Fill shell with damp potting soil, then sprinkle alfalfa or radish seed on top. Press seeds gently into dirt. Keep soil moist, but not wet. Set eggs on a sunny windowsill. Within a few days, seeds will sprout and grow green hair on the eggheads. Takes 5 to 8 days to grow a lush "head of hair." Most seeds germinate better if soaked 8 hours before planting. When sprouts are long enough, cut off and use in a salad.

Other Egg Tips

- If you add 2 tablespoons vinegar to water before cooking eggs, egg white from cracked eggs will not leak into the water.
- Puncture large end of eggshell with a needle just before cooking to keep eggs from cracking.
- Although fresh eggs can be stored in their cartons in the refrigerator for 2 to 3 weeks, hard-cooked eggs should be refrigerated when cooled and used within 1 week.

Egg Animals—Colored eggs make appealing Easter bunnies and chicks. Using the patterns below, cut out feet from orange posterboard for chicks or white posterboard for bunnies. Fold feet, bend narrow holding pieces, cut where indicated and slip edges into notches. Glue or tape to form circle-stand for egg. Place egg into circle. It should hold egg up. Make circles from tape and attach feet to egg bottom.

Cut bunnies' ears from white construction paper and chicks' beaks from orange construction paper. Attach ears by folding back flap and securing with tape. Use marking pens to draw eyes, nose, mouth and other details. Egg animals make delightful additions to your Easter table or cute gifts for young friends.

Easter-Bunny Cake

It's almost too cute to eat!

1 (8- or 9-inch) round cake, baked
4 cups white frosting
Decorative eyes and ears cut from paper plates
2 cups coconut, if desired
1 pink snowball cupcake

Cut cake in half. Frost one half and place other on top, flat edges together. Stand both sides up with flat cut edge on a cutting board or plate. Place some frosting under cake to secure it. Frost cake. Turn cake so round end faces you. Place eyes and bunny nose on rounded edge. Add ears, whiskers and snowball for tail. For coconut lovers, put coconut all over cake to make furry bunny.

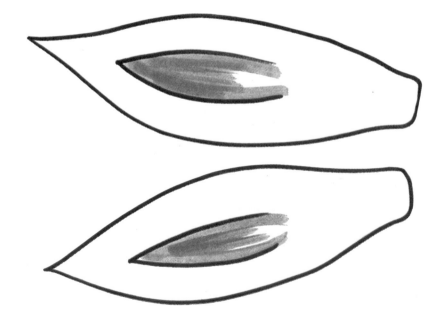

EGGS AND EASTER TREATS

Coloring Easter eggs is so much fun, the refrigerator may be packed with them when the holiday is over. Follow these suggestions and they'll be as tasty to eat as they were fun to create.

Big Freeze—Grate eggs and place portions in small freezer bags or cartons. Freeze for later use. Thawed, they provide excellent garnish for green salads. They taste good creamed over toast or added to casseroles.

Cold Meat Relish

A different relish treat.

2/3 to 1 cup mayonnaise
1/4 cup sweet pickle relish, drained
2 tablespoons parsley, finely chopped
1 teaspoon prepared mustard
3/4 cup grated frozen eggs, or 3 hard-cooked eggs
Salt and pepper to taste

Mix ingredients. Serve over cold meats as relish or sandwich spread. Makes 2 cups.

Use the following recipe to make delicious deviled eggs.

Deviled Eggs

A terrific way to prepare your eggs.

6 hard-cooked eggs, peeled
2 tablespoons butter or margarine, softened
3 tablespoons mayonnaise
1 tablespoon prepared mustard
Salt and pepper
Dash paprika
1/4 cup grated cheese, if desired

Cut eggs in half lengthwise and remove egg yolks. Mash yolks and combine with butter or margarine, mayonnaise and mustard. Season with salt and pepper. Stuff egg whites and sprinkle with paprika. Add 1/4 cup grated cheese to egg mixture for a great variation. Makes 12 halves.

APRIL FOOLS' CAPERS

What's April Fools' Day without tricks or pranks? Pull a few on family and friends with these nifty ideas.

- Insert a round piece of paper or posterboard into a few of your breakfast pancakes as you cook them.
- Set your children's and spouse's clock ahead one hour. Let everyone get up, eat breakfast and dress an hour early. Enjoy a fun April Fools' activity together during the extra time.
- Be backwards on April 1. Serve dinner in the morning and breakfast before bedtime. Start dinner with dessert, then entree and vegetable, ending with soup. Encourage everyone to eat with his left hand (or right hand for left-handers).
- Frost a square piece of Styrofoam as an April Fools' cake.

MEMORIAL DAY REMINISCING

The traditional Memorial Day is a day to remember soldiers who gave their lives in war. Today it is also a family holiday.

Pass on memories of your parents, grandparents and other family members with a Memorial Day "Show and Tell." Spend the afternoon talking about special relatives and visiting places you knew when you were a child. Describe games you played and the way you lived. Record your memories on cassette tapes as you talk. Dig out old photos and memorabilia. Concentrate on one individual or family per year.

FOURTH OF JULY GARDEN PARTY

Your guests will get a bang out of your next Fourth of July party when they sample this flower-basket buffet. It's easy, elegant and will be the highlight of the day's celebrations!

S M T W T F S
      1 2 3 4 5
 6 7 8 9 10 11 12
13 14 15 16 17 18 19
20 21 22 23 24 25 26
27 28 29 30 31

Flower-Basket Buffet—Create a make-your-own salad buffet no one will forget. To assemble, arrange clean, ready-to-eat vegetables in a large wicker flower basket. An 18x23'' basket is an ideal size. Starting at the back of the basket and working toward the front, arrange:

- Romaine lettuce. Cover outer edges of basket as well as the bottom to provide a beautiful green frame and backing.
- Several bunches of curly endive.
- Large, attractive cauliflower, flanked by 2 large red cabbages, cut in wedges.
- Several large green peppers with tops cut out and insides hollowed, filled with carrot sticks.
- Five bunches of radishes with bottoms trimmed.
- Fresh mushrooms attractively arranged.
- Cucumbers and tomatoes to fill gaps.
- Groups of scallions tied to basket handle with florist's wire.

Serve salad dressing, croutons and other salad ingredients in flowerpots lined with plastic wrap. Wrap plastic over the edge of the pot and secure with tape. Fill one pot with corn, another with thawed peas and a third with bread sticks. For a whimsical touch, tape seed packets to the ends of serving spoons you prop in flowerpotted vegetables. You may even want to make your own imaginative seed packets to label pots.

To serve your salad, place several sharp knives and pairs of kitchen scissors around the basket. Guests snip off greens and trimmings onto their own salad plates. They dish out other vegetables and dressings to complete their salads. A flower basket never looked prettier—or tasted better. Serves 15 to 20.

Flowerpot Grill—You'll need large, unglazed flowerpots at least 11 inches high and 11 inches wide for these portable, easy-to-use grills. Fill flowerpots with dirt or gravel to within 5 inches of the top. Cover dirt or gravel with a piece of foil so briquets do not settle into dirt and go out from lack of proper ventilation.

Place briquets in center of foil-lined pot and light. Allow 30 to 40 minutes before briquets are hot enough for guests to begin using them. Set a cooling rack or wire grill—not a refrigerator rack—over top of flowerpot and you're ready to cook.

Flowerpot Kebobs—Near flowerpot grills, set up a line of plastic-lined flowerpots filled with kebob ingredients. For meat kebobs, precook or marinate meat. Fill flowerpots with small cubes of tender beef cuts, cherry tomatoes, mushrooms, small onions, green pepper chunks and other ingredients.

Place bamboo skewers on table so guests can assemble kebobs. If you have trouble with food flopping to its heavy sides when turning over, thread food on double skewer. Provide barbecue or marinating sauces so guests can brush sauce over meat-and-vegetable kebobs.

Try fruit kebobs as well. Use pineapple chunks, maraschino cherries, banana chunks, orange sections and peach chunks to make kebobs. Heat for a few minutes on grill after assembling.

Dian shows Tom what to put in an Over-The-Seat Car Game Organizer.

Traveling

6

Traveling together as a family can be a harrowing experience. It's hard to get everything organized, remember all the odds and ends, even decide where you're going to go.

The information provided in this chapter will help you have a better vacation, from planning your itinerary to travel preparation. Use these ideas to make your vacation the best experience possible. Create a fun vacation the entire family will enjoy.

TRAVELING EASY

Whether you go on short trips or long treks, these tools are designed to help you organize your travel. They can make your trips more carefree and add to your enjoyment.

TRAVEL PREPARATION

Looseleaf Travel Organizer—A looseleaf notebook with pocket dividers can help you keep track of important papers, maps and brochures. It also allows you to record thoughts and impressions for future reference.

- Keep maps in the front pocket for easy access. When you no longer need a map, place it in the back pocket.
- Label one pocket divider for each city, national park or area you will be visiting.
- Arrange dividers in the order of your itinerary. Place brochures, pamphlets, information sheets and tourist aids in appropriate pockets.
- Make a list of hotels, restaurants, sights and activities you've planned at the destination. Include addresses and phone numbers of friends and relatives you plan to contact.
- Include pockets for credit purchases, records of gas mileage and car expenses, a list of people to send picture postcards to along the way, tickets, reservations and other important papers.

Traveling High Chair—Have a high chair ready when you travel or go visiting. You'll be able to slide your child up to almost any table. You'll need:

    1 large bath towel
    1 pkg. 2-inch seam binding
    2 yards 1-inch grosgrain ribbon or cord
    Scissors, thread and pins

Use standard dining or kitchen chair to help construct this seat. Lay bath towel over chair with 6 inches hanging down back. Pin towel on each side. Test to see if towel can easily slip off chair. Sew sides together.

After sewing, place towel on chair and let the rest of it hang down the front of chair and over seat. Set child on seat. Bring towel up around legs. Cut both sides of towel in half circles to resemble legs of baby plastic pants. See pattern. If towel is too long, trim to fit child at his waist. Finish raw edge around legs with seam binding.

Attach 1 yard grosgrain ribbon or cord on each corner of seat. Pull strings up. Tie around child and secure to back of chair. You're ready to seat your child whenever you're away from home.

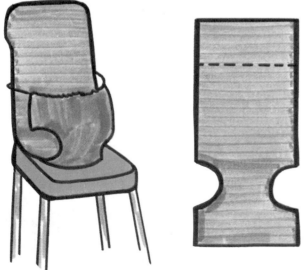

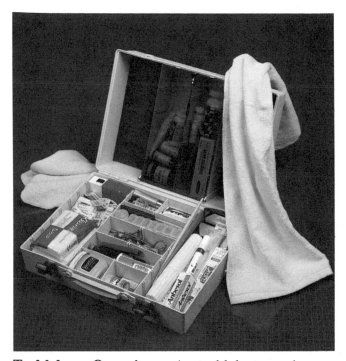

Vacation Care For Houseplants—When going away on vacation, take steps to keep plants healthy. Water plants thoroughly. Completely cover pot and soil with plastic wrap. The plastic forms an airtight container or miniature greenhouse around plant. This method keeps soil moist for up to 2 weeks.

Another way to keep plants watered is to use watering wicks. Run cotton cord or commercial water wick about 2 inches deep into plant's soil. Run other end into a container of water slightly lower than the top of the pot. The wick will gradually feed water to the plant while you're away.

Tacklebox Organizer—A tacklebox makes a handy organizer for small items. Small boxes hold individual supplies. A large box will hold the entire family's toiletries. Tape list of contents inside lid for a quick check-off for packing and repacking. Use tacklebox for organizing personal items such as cosmetics, toiletries, medicines and emergency supplies. Fill other compartments with supplies everyone uses, such as first-aid supplies, needle and thread, tissues, aspirin and shampoo.

Window Eraser—Keep a new, clean chalkboard eraser handy to wipe the inside of windows when moisture collects on them.

Emergency Precautions—Just in case! Apply large strips of fluorescent tape diagonally across inside top of your car trunk. If you need to stop on the highway, open your trunk and you have a warning sign. You can also put tape on an old hunting vest or a vest made from a garbage bag. Use emergency vest when repairing auto on highway.

TRAVEL ORGANIZERS

You can make family travel more relaxing if children are occupied and entertained. Organizing games and activities can be easy and fun with these simple suggestions.

Over-The-Seat Car Game Organizer—Make a travel activity organizer to slip over the back of the front car seat. Buy a flat, transparent lingerie organizer. Attach enough cord to each of four corners so top ties hang over front seat. Bottom ties come through front seat like seat belts. Tie bottom and top ties together. Organizer hangs down back of front seat. Transparent pockets hold games and supplies for riders during trips. You can also use an old shoebag or make one to save money.

Fill Your Organizer—Carry anything you consider handy, useful or necessary to make your trip more enjoyable. Here are a few suggestions:

Children's Activities
    Binoculars, magnifying glass
    Colored pencils or markers
    Lined paper, art paper,
        construction paper
    Scissors (blunt-point)
    Card games
    Wallet and play money
    Small toys such as play watch,
        dolls, cars, jewelry, storybook
        glove puppets
    Felt tic-tac-toe game
    Small magnetic checkers

Teen or Adult Activities
    Calculator
    Stationery, stamps, postcards,
        address book
    Card games
    Camera and flash
    Miniature pocket games
    Tissues, mirror, comb, lip balm

General Travel Supplies
    Disposable washcloths
    Paper towels
    Granola bars
    Toilet paper, tissues
    Garbage bags
    Sewing kit
    First-aid kit
    Insect spray
    Paper plates and cups
    Plastic flatware
    Napkins
    Plastic tablecloth
    Towel

APRON ORGANIZER

Here's a simple idea for making a super-neat organizer! A bath towel and length of cord will make a handy, multi-pocketed apron for keeping items convenient when you need to use them.

1. Fold up one end of towel about 5 inches.
2. To measure pockets, place items to be carried in fold.
3. Pin pocket seams.
4. Take out items and sew pockets.
5. For shallow pockets, make seam across bottom 1 to 2 inches up from fold. This blocks off unneeded portions. Don't make pockets too shallow or items will drop out.
6. To make casing, fold top of towel over about 5 inches above top of pockets. Place cord inside fold with equal amount of cord hanging loose on both sides. Stitch across towel below cord.

USES FOR APRON ORGANIZERS

Auto Repair Apron—Buy an extra-large, dark-colored towel, matching hand towel and cord. Fold extra-large towel in half. Make drawstring casing. To make pockets, lay hand towel lengthwise 4 inches down from casing on bottom side of extra-large towel. Measure pockets to hold commonly used car-repair tools: screwdrivers, socket wrench, heavy work gloves, pliers, flashlight. Sew around three sides of hand towel and down each pocket. Attach Velcro fasteners or ties to top of towel to fasten around neck. Towel will protect clothes as you make repairs.

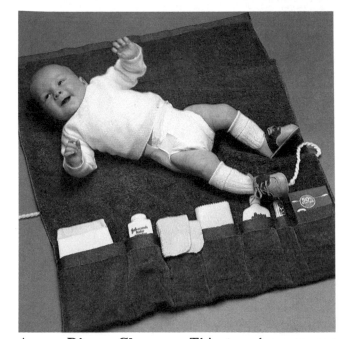

Apron Diaper-Changer—This travel apron can be a lifesaver. Fit pockets to supplies needed for changing baby. Include toy to distract baby and plastic bags for disposing soiled diapers. If you find yourself in a place where you must lay baby on an unclean surface, spread out entire towel with pockets near you. Lay baby on towel for cleanliness and protection.

Grooming Apron—Measure pockets to hold grooming tools. Towel above drawstring hangs over pocket as a handy wipe for hands and face. Make aprons for children from smaller towels. Decorate with child's name or name of tool. Aprons help children keep regular grooming habits and bedtime routine when away from home.

CHILDREN'S TRAVEL ACTIVITIES

With imagination and a few resources, you can keep children busy on long trips. Try some of the following games, equipment and activities.

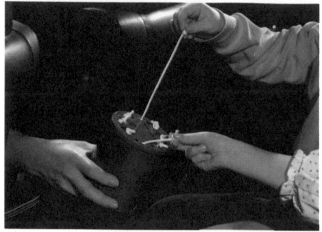

Decision-Making Can—This simple device can help make decisions and settle arguments. You'll need an empty can with a plastic lid and cotton cord. Using a paper punch, punch holes equal distances apart in lid. Cut cord into unequal lengths. The number of cords must match the number of holes.

Put one cord through each hole and tie a knot at both ends. Pull cords so only knots show on top of lid. Place cords in can as you place lid on.

To make a decision, the arbitrator has each player pick a knot and pull gently until his cord reaches the end. The player choosing the longest cord makes the decision.

Each time cords have been pulled, have an adult pull them back to former positions. Turn lid so holes are in different positions.

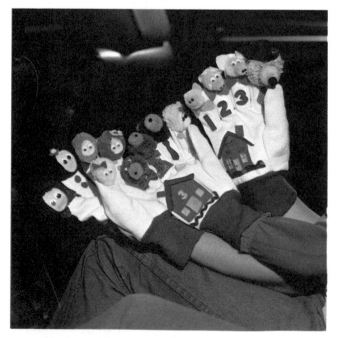

Pillow Lapboard—Make a handy lapboard that can be used as a pillow, too. You'll need:

12x18'' Masonite board
1 pillow
1 pillow case
1-1/2 yards Velcro

Pillow provides a lapboard that doesn't slip. It's the right height for writing and games. Pillow is attached by Velcro on 3 sides to lapboard. Child can store books and crayons between board and pillow. Board can be turned over when child is tired and the pillow used for a comfortable nap.

Glove-Finger Puppets—Young children love seeing favorite fairy tales dramatized. Goldilocks and the Three Bears, Cinderella, Little Red Riding Hood and others come alive with finger puppets.

To make puppets, purchase inexpensive gloves. Each finger will be a different character of the story. Buy enough small pompons, felt and other materials to create each character. Use colors such as brown for bears and gold for Goldilocks. Glue pompons to top of glove finger for each character. Use eyes and other craft supplies for features. Illustrate a different story with each glove.

Slip on glove and wriggle appropriate fingers to animate characters as you tell the story.

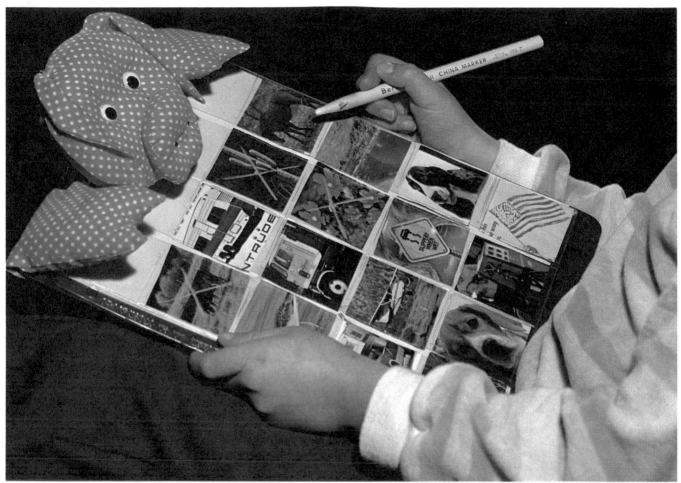

Sunshine Certificates— Make up special certificates to be presented each day of your trip. Make certificates look official by adding ribbon and gold seals purchased at a stationery store. Recipient can exchange certificate for special privilege after you return from your vacation.

Some sample certificates might include:

Good Disposition Award for person who complained least during the day. Good for one night at the movies with a friend.

Merry Sunshine Award for family member who didn't argue during the day. Good for special time with a friend.

Certificate of Sanitation for person who kept cleanest. Good for one night out with Dad.

Certificate of Helpfulness for family member who did his share and more without being asked. Good for an evening out with Mom.

Travel Bingo—Make your own versatile travel bingo. Use clear-plastic slide pages with multiple square pockets. Purchase these pages at a photography store. Use bottom 4 rows of pockets to make a square. In pockets place small pictures cut from magazines or made by children. Choose items children can spot from the car such as trucks, farm animals, buildings, signs—even words appearing on billboards.

To play, children mark an X with a grease pencil on plastic pocket containing picture of an item they spot. Winner is first person to find all the pictures in a straight or diagonal line on his sheet. Erase sheets with a damp tissue or rag. Scramble pictures for a new game or have children trade pictures.

CLOSE-TO-HOME VACATIONS

Just because you are low on money this year doesn't mean you have to give up your vacation. Here are some fun close-to-home vacation ideas.

Backyard Vacations—If your travel budget has dwindled to nothing, you can still have an exciting vacation in your own backyard. Rent a videotape machine and camera and make your own "movie," complete with script, props and costumes. Try a melodrama, mystery, cowboy epic or family drama. Everyone can participate and share the fun. A family documentary can also serve as a valuable and entertaining keepsake.

One-Day Mystery Excursions—Designate each member of the family as person-in-charge for a particular day of your vacation. Within your travel budget, that person decides where you'll go, what you'll do and where you'll eat. Person-in-charge chooses whether or not to reveal the plans before the family begins the day.

Be Daring—If you're having trouble deciding where to go, hang up a map of the area in which you're interested. Blindfold a member of your travel group. Have that person walk toward map and stick a pin in it. Travel to the pinpoint location and explore the area.

Ethnic Experience—If you can't visit a foreign country, learn about one! Have an ethnic day. Choose a country and culture to learn about. Serve an ethnic meal like you would eat in that country. Ask different family members to tell about the country's culture. One might select music; another might check out books from the library on the country and read to the family. Let each family member choose a country and plan an ethnic day around it.

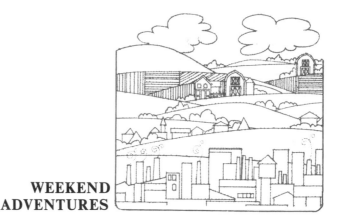

WEEKEND ADVENTURES

With gas prices climbing and inflation cutting into vacation savings, dreams of cruises and expensive tours fade. The following alternative vacations can be as exciting as a dreamed-of tour or cruise, without great expense. These vacations require a minimum of travel and a day or two of time. Designed for fun, they can be adapted to any budget.

Industrial Treasures—Make arrangements to tour a factory or interesting business in your community. Many factories give educational tours if you arrange them ahead of time. Here are some tours you might enjoy:

Steel plant, generator plant or tire-making plant
Bakery
Telephone company
Furniture-manufacturing plant
Auto-assembly plant
Newspaper

Play Tourist—Check into a motel in a nearby city or tourist area. Visit tourist spots. Take your camera to make a visual diary of your visit.

Nature Days—Contact a nearby office of the National Park Service or U.S. Forest Service. Obtain a list of local nature walks, hiking trails or interesting walks. Pack a picnic lunch and spend the day walking and appreciating nature. Stretch your stay into a two- or three-day camping or backpacking trip when you find an area you like.

Farm/Ranch Weekend—Contact an extension agent at your state land-grant college. Ask about interesting agricultural areas you may tour. Different areas of the country will offer different kinds of agricultural activities. You might consider:

Turkey farms
Poultry farms/egg processing plants
Cheese factories
Vineyards
Cattle ranches
Harvest time on a ranch or farm

Relive History—Every community contains hidden historical treasures: old buildings, sites of important events or museums full of artifacts. Your state historical society or local Chamber of Commerce can tell you about famous and little-known spots of historical interest in your area.

Recreational Shopping—Spend a weekend visiting local auctions, flea markets, antique shops or garage sales. You can have fun looking without buying. You may discover a treasure among the items for sale.

Bike Hike—Bicycle to a picnic spot. For a longer trek, bike to town for lunch or sightseeing. Check the Chamber of Commerce for bike trails. Many trails offer interesting sights and are designed for bicycling safety.

Weekend Grab-And-Run Box—Create your own grab-and-run box of equipment and supplies you'll need for a spontaneous day or weekend of fun. Your box might contain:

> Personal items for everyone: toothbrushes, toothpaste, soap
> Washcloth (in a plastic bag for quick cleanups)
> Towels, bathing suits and beachballs
> Sports equipment such as softball, bat, Frisbee and football
> Camera and film
> Paper plates, cups, napkins, plastic utensils and tablecloth
> Pillows and blankets
> Two-days' supply of nonperishable food, recipes and cooking equipment
> 3x5 card listing perishable food to complete recipes. You can pick up foods as needed.

Weekend Destination Box—Spend an evening with family or friends discussing nearby spots to visit. List the activities you would like to enjoy on weekends in the next few months. Write each destination and activity on a separate slip of paper. Place slips in a box or bowl. On each free weekend, draw a slip from your destination box and enjoy that trip or activity.

RESEARCHING VACATIONS

To find new and exciting places to go or sights to see, you may need to gather some information. Ways to find this information are listed below.

- Write or call:
  U.S. Travel Service
  U.S. Department of Commerce
  Washington, D.C. 20230
  (202) 377-4853/4987
  Ask for information on specific states or locations you're thinking about visiting.
- Check with a local travel agency. Most schedule vacations at no cost to you. Many can save you money with discounts for airlines and hotels.
- Visit your public library and check their travel resources.
- Magazines on travel, camping, backpacking and recreational vehicles often contain articles and advertisements full of information.
- Organizations such as the American Automobile Association provide valuable information about travel alternatives, routes and reservations.
- Each state, and many cities, have an office promoting tourism. Locate the office by mailing an information request to the governor's office of the state you want to visit.

Jane and Dian discuss ways children can use Umbrella Tent.

Kids' Treats
7

Kids need lots of time and attention to grow up healthy and happy. This chapter is full of imaginative ways to help your kids have fun as they grow.

Encourage children to eat more nutritiously by making good food fun. Let them participate in making the food. They may not even notice it's good for them!

Creative activities, costumes and puppet play can enlarge your child's world. Make-believe expands the imagination. Allow children to help you with the projects—they'll enjoy it more!

FOODS DESIGNED WITH KIDS IN MIND

Here are some super treats for kids. They're easy to make and fun to eat. Try them—your kids will love eating nutritiously.

Ice-Cream Cones—Serve potato or gelatin salad in an ice-cream cone. Children can eat salad more easily. Cones make salad a treat to eat.

Hard-Roll Sandwich—Hollow out the center of a hard roll. Fill roll with chicken, egg or tuna salad filling. Sandwich can be eaten without filling oozing out.

Make Food Spillproof—Instead of serving tacos with loose meat that spills out easily, cook ground beef in a log-shape roll. Wrap meat in lettuce leaf and thin slice of cheese. Slip rolled-up food into taco shell. Larger piece keeps food from spilling on children's clothing.

Serve Kid-Size Portions—Choose a small apple or orange. Or quarter a large apple and offer child one quarter at a time.

Use Pocket Breads—Instead of separate bread slices for tuna or chicken sandwiches, try pita bread. Add alfalfa or bean sprouts to give sandwiches added nutrition and crunch.

FOODS WITH PERSONALITY

Make familiar shapes out of children's foods. It's fun, especially when you create interesting foods to look at. Here are some quick, easy ideas.

Peanut-Butter Pizza—If you'd like something fun to prepare for lunch, try peanut-butter pizza. Make your favorite homemade or packaged pizza crust and bake. Spread crust with peanut butter mixed with honey. Top with raisins, banana slices, walnuts, pineapple chunks and coconut.

Sprinkle coarsely grated mozzarella cheese over pizza. Bake in oven until cheese melts. Slice and serve.

Individual Pizza Faces—With supervision, children can make pizza people. Spread pizza sauce over English-muffin halves. Arrange bits of cooked sausage, pepperoni cut in shapes, tomato, green pepper, onion or mushroom slices to form faces on top of sauce. Sprinkle creations with grated mozzarella or Parmesan cheese. Broil briefly to warm. They're ready to eat!

Painted Toast—Use food coloring in milk to paint faces or cartoons on bread. Put 1/4 cup milk in a glass. Add a few drops of food coloring and stir. With a clean brush, let children create designs. Toast and serve as part of sandwich.

Egg Sailboats—Cut peeled, hard-cooked egg in half lengthwise. Have children cut a slice of American cheese in half diagonally to form a triangle. Skewer each triangular cheese sail onto toothpick mast. Secure mast onto egg boat.

Egg Posy—Cut peeled, hard-cooked egg into thin, round slices. Allow children to arrange slices in circular flower pattern with egg-slice petals overlapping slightly. Spoon favorite salad dressing in middle of egg-slice circle as center of flower. Cut square slice of American cheese as leaves. Add thin slice of toast for stem. Attach stem and leaves to egg flower.

Strawberry Surprise

Delicious strawberry slush.

1 (10-oz.) pkg. frozen strawberries,
   partially thawed
1/2 cup milk
1/4 cup sugar
1 qt. strawberry yogurt

Blend strawberries and milk until smooth. Add sugar and yogurt. Blend all ingredients on low speed until thick and smooth. Makes a slush. Serve immediately. Serves 4 to 6.

Big-Foot Hot Dog—Cut hot dog lengthwise so it opens flat. Cut in half. Arrange pieces on hamburger bun so rounded ends peek out to form toes. Let children add tomato slices, cheese, onions and pickle relish, along with favorite spreads. Heat until cheese begins to melt.

Peach Pleaser

Use fresh or canned peaches for this treat.

1 (16-oz.) can peaches or 2 cups sliced,
   fresh peaches
1 cup milk
1 pt. vanilla ice cream, slightly softened
1/2 teaspoon almond flavoring
1 (6-oz.) can frozen orange-juice concentrate

Mix all ingredients in blender until smooth. Serves 6.

Sandwich Faces—Make these open-face sandwiches on bread or English-muffin halves.
- Peanut-butter sandwich with olive eyes, nut nose, tangerine ears and cheese-puff mouth.
- Hamburger patty with pickle ears, catsup nose, cheese tie, pepper eyebrows and olive eyes.
- Sloppy Joe with grated-cheese hair, olive eyes, green pepper mouth, and mushroom nose and ears.

Purple Cow

Great on a hot day!

2 cups vanilla ice cream, slightly softened
3 tablespoons frozen grape-juice concentrate,
   thawed
1 cup milk

Put grape-juice concentrate and milk in blender. Process until smooth. Add softened ice cream and beat at low speed. Serve immediately. Serves 4.

Oatmeal Bars

No baking required!

1/2 cup butter or margarine
1/2 cup packed brown sugar
1 teaspoon grated orange peel
1/2 cup orange juice
2 tablespoons wheat germ
2 cups rolled oats (quick-cooking oats are best)
1 cup toasted flaked coconut
1/2 cup chopped nuts
1/4 cup sesame seeds, if desired

Melt butter or margarine in saucepan. Add brown sugar, orange peel and orange juice. Stir until sugar is dissolved. Add wheat germ, rolled oats, coconut and nuts. Add sesame seeds, if desired. Spread in 9-inch-square pan and refrigerate until hard. Cut into squares. Makes 36 bars.

Silly Salads—These salads should appeal to any child. Make rocket salad by cutting a peeled banana in half. Stand upright in pineapple ring. Trim top of rocket with maraschino cherries. Decorate pineapple rocket base with shredded carrots or cheese for flames.

Raisins in cheese or peanut-butter-filled celery stick can be ants on a log.

Nest pear-half on lettuce leaves for a cute bunny. Add miniature marshmallow ears and tail with raisin eyes.

Make a reindeer from peach-half. Add prune ears, raisin eyes and a cherry nose. It may entice a child into trying food he does not normally like.

Make other foods into faces by using carrot and celery sticks for bodies; olives, cherries, grapes and strawberries for eyes; shredded cheese, carrots and coconut for hair; and alphabet cereal for letters to write names.

Gingersnap Yummies

The kids can help with this treat.

3/4 cup shortening
1-1/3 cups sugar
1 egg
1/4 cup light molasses
2 teaspoons baking soda
2 cups all-purpose flour
1/4 teaspoon salt
1 teaspoon ground cinnamon
1 teaspoon ground cloves
1 teaspoon ground ginger

Cream shortening with 1 cup sugar. Add egg and molasses. Beat well. Mix in remaining ingredients, except 1/3 cup sugar. Children can shape dough into small balls. Dip or roll balls in 1/3 cup sugar and place on baking sheet. Bake 10 to 12 minutes in a 375F (190C) oven. Makes 24 to 36 cookies.

Fruit Candy

A mixture of fruit tastes great.

**2 lbs. fruit, such as dried apricots, apples,
 dates, raisins and figs
Juice and peel of 1 orange
1 cup walnuts, coarsely chopped
1 or 2 tablespoons honey or corn syrup, if needed
1 (6-oz.) pkg. chocolate pieces, if desired**

Grind fruit and orange peel together using meat grinder with medium blade. Don't grind too finely. Stir in orange juice and nuts. Taste. If you want candy sweeter, blend in 1 or 2 tablespoons honey or corn syrup. Shape into balls or bars. Let stand 24 hours. If desired, melt chocolate pieces in double boiler. Spread melted chocolate on top of each ball or bar. Makes 24.

Nutty Putty

They can play with it and eat it!

**3-1/2 cups peanut butter
4 cups powdered sugar
3-1/2 cups corn syrup or honey
4 cups dried milk powder
1 (6-oz.) pkg. chocolate pieces, if desired**

Mix first four ingredients together. Divide into 10 to 15 portions. Dip into melted chocolate pieces for a tasty snack. Store extra portions in plastic bags in refrigerator or freezer.

This treat can serve as fun dough. With clean hands, children can mold and shape into animals, flowers and other objects while they eat it.

HOMEMADE TOYS

It's a special treat for children to make their own toys. The following toys provide loads of fun and are usually made from discards or common household items.

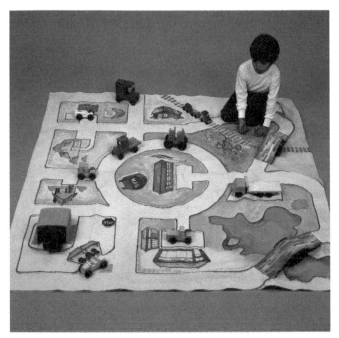

Places In Your Neighborhood

**Large (at least 2x3') piece of
 plain-colored denim, sailcloth or canvas
Fabric paints, liquid embroidery markers or
 fabric and felt scraps for appliqué**

This flat town, complete with roads, airport, shopping center, homes and other familiar buildings, will occupy children for hours. To make town, hem all sides of fabric. Draw features you want in your town. Include roads, your home and children's favorite places like school, candy store, library, Grandma's, and Dad's or Mom's work. Mark and color features with fabric paints or markers. Children will enjoy driving toy cars and trucks on streets of their town.

Variation: Draw cowboy setting with corral, bunkhouse, waterhole, Indian village and fort. Supply children with plastic cowboys, Indians, cavalrymen, covered wagons and wild broncos.

Waterbed Bounce—Use an old rubber waterbed mattress for a trampoline. Find a flat, safe spot. Fill bed with water and start bouncing. If used on a lawn, move waterbed regularly so grass is not damaged.

Indoor Miniature Golf—Set up your own indoor golf course in your family room or living room. You will need:

- Traps and obstacles (small odd-shaped boxes, cans with both ends cut out, small pillows, throw rugs and other obstacles)
- Putter (3" length of a 1-inch dowel with hole drilled to fit 1/2-inch dowel 30" long)
- Whiffle or PG Balls (practice balls)

Use your imagination to think of household items to make your own miniature golf course. Place obstacles to putt around, under, over and through. One enterprising family placed one hole so players had to putt through a tin-can tunnel, up a cardboard ramp, across a board and down around a pillow to the hole. Lowest number of strokes wins.

Fingerpaints

1/2 cup granular clothes starch
1/2 cup cold water
1 qt. boiling water
1/2 cup soap flakes
Few drops of food coloring

Soften starch in cold water. Add boiling water and stir in soap flakes. Blend with mixer on medium speed. Pour into small jars and add different food color to each jar and stir. Use on butcher paper or other slick paper for best results.

Toothpick-Pea Building—For hours of creative entertainment, make a toothpick-pea building. Soak a package of pea seeds for 8 hours. Use peas to join toothpicks together to make your "building."

Fun Dough

1 cup all-purpose flour
1 tablespoon salad oil
1/2 cup salt
1/2 cup cold water
2 teaspoons cream of tartar
Few drops of food coloring

Mix all ingredients in saucepan. Stirring constantly, heat dough 2 to 3 minutes until thick. Cool. Store in heavy airtight container. Makes 1-1/2 cups.

Frozen Water Fountain—To make a refreshing water fountain, use a thermos with a spout. Fill thermos with cold water and ice cubes. Turn on spout and drink from "fountain." Put it outside in the shady part of children's play area. Hang from a tree limb or fence at convenient height for a child. Children can help themselves. It is also great for adults who are working outside in the heat.

Egg-Carton Adding Toss

2 egg cartons
Marking pens
Pennies
12" of cord

This simple game takes only a few pennies to play. Cut bottom section from 1 or 2 egg cartons. With marking pen, mark random numbers from 1 to 12 on bottom of each individual compartment. Place cartons on floor or table. Place cord on floor as throwing line 2 to 5 feet from cartons. Children take turns standing behind cord and throwing pennies into egg carton sections. To compute score, child must add numbers under his pennies. Each child keeps a running total of his score. First to reach 100 (or any score set) wins. This game helps children learn or review math skills.

Variation: Have children toss 2 pennies, then multiply numbers. Add points after 5 to 10 rounds for total score.

Chinese Jump Rope—For entertainment and to improve your child's coordination, try a Chinese jump rope. It's an individual activity; no one is required to hold the ends of the rope. You will need:

    1 pkg. 1/4-inch elastic
    2 chairs or other objects with enough weight to hold elastic taut

Place elastic around chair or object. Leave at least 1 foot between elastic. Adjust, cut elastic and tie a knot. Child jumps, using sequences at right or ones she makes up.

As the child becomes more skilled, move elastic higher up the chair leg, making it more difficult to jump.

Bean-Bag Throw

1 large cardboard box
Fabric or felt scraps
Dried beans

Make bean bags by folding and sewing little pillows from fabric scraps. Fill with beans and sew opening closed.

Cut openings of various sizes and shapes in one side of box. Make openings large enough for bean bags to go through. Take turns throwing bean bags into box openings. Vary game by giving more points for hitting smaller openings or for tossing accurately from greater distance.

CHINESE JUMP ROPE

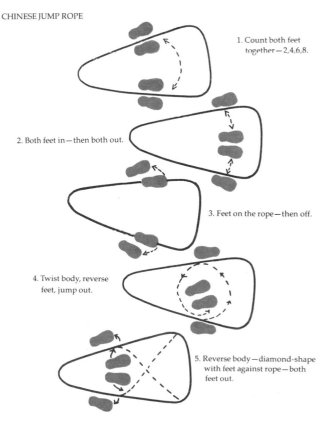

1. Count both feet together—2,4,6,8.

2. Both feet in—then both out.

3. Feet on the rope—then off.

4. Twist body, reverse feet, jump out.

5. Reverse body—diamond-shape with feet against rope—both feet out.

RAINY-DAY ACTIVITIES

When weather forces children inside, parents, sitters and children can make their own fun. These inexpensive activities provide a maximum of fun with a minimum of preparation and money. Creating art from household objects and supplies can help make a rainy day hard to forget.

FUN ACTIVITIES

These activities will keep your kids busy for hours, especially on a rainy day. Try them and you can have fun being a kid again yourself.

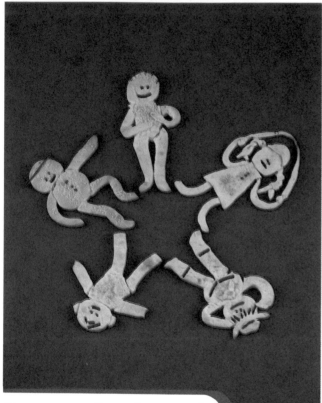

Sesame-Seed People

1 (7-1/2-oz.) pkg. refrigerator biscuits
1/4 cup all-purpose flour
1/2 cup butter or margarine
1/2 cup sesame seeds
Licorice ropes (red and black)

On lightly floured surface, roll out refrigerator biscuits about 1/8-inch thick. Cut dough into strips and shapes. Let children press strips together to form stick people. Use butter or margarine on one side of stick people and place on baking sheet. Butter tops and sprinkle with sesame seeds. Cut pieces of licorice ropes for mouths, hair and other features. Press into dough. Bake at 400F (205C) 8 to 10 minutes until golden brown. Makes 4 to 6 stick people.

Pudding Fingerpainting

1 (3-3/4-oz.) pkg. instant pudding
2 cups milk
Butcher paper, or other smooth-surface paper

Mix instant pudding according to package directions. Place 2 to 3 tablespoons on butcher paper or other shiny, smooth-surface paper. After washing hands, children can fingerpaint in pudding, making designs and drawings.

Hippo Roll

1 lb. ready-made frozen bread dough
2 raisins
Toothpicks
2 tablespoons butter or margarine, melted

While dough is still semi-frozen, with kitchen scissors, cut 1-inch of dough off loaf. Divide this piece into 4 legs. Shape body of hippopotamus with large piece of dough. Dip small pieces of dough in water and attach legs to body. Use raisins for eyes. Cut mouth and prop open with toothpicks while baking.

Bake 20 to 30 minutes in 400F (205C) oven until golden brown. As bread comes out of oven, brush with melted butter or margarine. Makes 1 hippo.

Spoon Dolls—Use a wooden spoon to make a doll for decorating gifts or as a present itself. The bowl of the spoon becomes the doll's head. Use furry fabric, string or yarn for hair, a bow for color and a triangular piece of fabric for clothes. Tie bow at base of spoon and glue clothes on handle.

A wooden spoon doll attached to a present will add a special touch to the gift.

Indoor Croquet

4 to 8 empty shortening cans, open on both ends
4 to 8 sheets construction paper
Black marking pen
Tennis or ping-pong balls
Croquet mallets

To set up indoor croquet, cut 1x3'' strips from construction paper. Cut as many strips as you have cans. Write successive numbers (1, 2, 3 and so on) on top of each strip. Paste number strips on cans.

Place cans on sides and arrange around room. Children take turns hitting tennis or ping-pong balls with croquet mallet through cans in numerical order. First child to successfully hit through all cans wins.

Ar-Tee Shirts

1 sheet scratch paper
1 pencil with eraser
White or plain-colored tee-shirt
3 to 6 different-colored permanent magic markers
Acrylic paint

Let children and teenagers draw favorite cartoon characters or monsters on scratch paper. It may take a few tries to get drawing perfect. Go over design with black marker so you can see it through tee-shirt. Place design under front of tee-shirt and transfer with permanent black marker. Put a piece of heavy cardboard inside the shirt to keep markers from soaking through to the back. If you can't see through the shirt, make design with a fabric pencil on paper and iron it on the shirt. Be sure the sketch is backward if you use the fabric pencil. Let child finish coloring shirt with permanent markers and acrylic paint.

WORLD OF PUPPET PLAY

Making your own puppets and stage is another fun way to spend an afternoon.

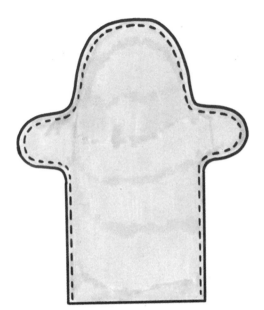

Fold-Up Puppet Stage

1 large cardboard appliance box
Spray paint and poster paints
Construction paper
Glue
1/2 yard (approximately) colorful fabric
Cord or twine
Straight-edged razor blade or knife

Choose a box such as a tall refrigerator box. Use razor blade or knife to cut box according to picture. Cut stage opening from front side.

Paint to hide lettering on box. Construct stage curtain by cutting length of material 1-1/2 times wider and about 2-1/2 inches longer than stage opening. Cut material in half lengthwise to form two vertical curtains. Fold top over cord and stitch casing. After stage is painted, knot and attach ends of casing or cord to stage so curtain hangs across stage opening. Use your puppets in this handy puppet stage!

Washcloth Puppets—Make pattern from brown paper bag according to illustration above. Use 2 washcloths for this puppet. Place one washcloth on top of the other. Put bottom of pattern along washcloth edge and pin on pattern. Cut and sew around puppet shape, leaving bottom open. Turn right-side out. Help children cut features from scraps and glue on washcloth. Children may want to paint or glue one face on one side of puppet and a different face on other side.

Sesame Street Play—When weather keeps children indoors, help them put on their own Sesame Street program. Children choose one letter and one number to spotlight. They can have fun finding objects beginning with their letter. Number spotlights provide fun, too. If they choose to spotlight "5" they can assemble 5 shoes and 5 cups. Using puppets, costumes or simple imagination, they can impersonate their favorite Sesame Street characters and act out their own drama.

Fluffy Slipper Puppet—Fluffy, furry slippers come in all sizes and make charming hand puppets. Purchase slippers the size of child's hand. To make puppet, fold slipper so sole doubles back to form puppet's mouth. Child places fingers where toes would normally go and thumb in heel to make puppet talk. Create features by cutting floppy or stand-up ears, tongue, fangs, teeth, eyes and lashes from felt and fabric scraps. Construct bulbous stuffed nose or fake-fur eyebrows. Glue on facial features.

Simple Sock Puppets—Socks make fun puppets. Children can stick hands in socks and stuff toe back to form face and mouth. Tack puppet's mouth with needle and thread. Draw eyes and nose on part of sock normally over foot. Or sew on button eyes and felt nostrils. A red tongue adds a clever accent.

PLAYTIME INSIDE

Sometimes it's hard to keep the kids entertained when they're stuck in the house. Try these ideas and they'll have fun for hours.

Indian Village

Paper-towel tube
Plain white paper cups, cone-shaped (or white paper car-oil funnels)
Paper
Toothpicks
Plastic Indian braves and ponies
Marking pens
Construction paper
Glue
Scissors

Children will enjoy constructing their own Indian village. Make teepees by decorating cone-shaped paper cups with Indian symbols and poking 2 to 3 pieces of toothpicks through point to form poles. Cut small slit up one side from wide end of cup and fold back for entrance. Paint some cups green, setting them around village as pine trees. Make totem pole from cardboard tube decorated with faces, paws and wings cut from construction paper. Plastic Indians and ponies complete a fun and colorful Indian village.

Going Fishing

1 large sheet of posterboard
1 (20-oz.) pkg. paraffin wax
10 to 20 paperclips
24" stick or dowel
18" of string
Small magnet

Cut 10 to 20 fish from posterboard. Melt paraffin in double boiler. Dip cardboard fish into paraffin until well-coated. Dry on waxed paper. Attach paperclip to front of each fish. Construct fishing pole by securing string to end of stick or dowel. Tie small magnet to end of string. Float wax-covered, paperclip fish in bathtub or large container. Children take turns fishing with magnet fishing pole to catch fish. Child catching most fish wins.

Variation: Write numbers on side of each fish before dipping in paraffin. Children add or multiply numbers of fish they catch to get total score at end of game. This helps children learn arithmetic.

Umbrella Play Tent—A piece of rope, a large umbrella and one or two shower curtains provide children with a portable outdoor play tent. It's ideal for playing in backyard, park or campsite. Hang umbrella in the shade, handle up, by securing it with rope to an overhanging branch. Attach shower curtain(s) to umbrella by slipping curtain holes onto protruding umbrella ribs. Overlap 2 to 4 holes to provide doors.

Let children decorate tent. Make simple outlines by cutting silhouettes from lightweight cardboard or foam meat-packing or bakery-packing trays. To make tent perpetual fun, buy smooth-surfaced, transparent shower curtain(s). Let children decorate them with wipe-off magic markers. At end of day when you take down tent, let them wipe off decorations with a cloth. Each time they play, children can transform their tent into a circus tent, fairy castle or gangster hideaway.

Variation: Use this tent as a portable dressing room. Kids can change clothes in it before and after running through sprinkler or playing in wading pools. It'll keep indoor carpeting and floors dry.

Card-Table House—Transform an ordinary card table into an imaginative house, cave or tent with 4-1/3 yards of 45-inch-wide muslin or other cotton fabric and some fasteners.

Cut pieces for card-table house. Measure your card table and cut a piece to cover the top of the table. It should hang over the edge 5/8'' for a 5/8-inch seam. Cut 4 pieces of fabric large enough to cover each side from the top of the table to the floor. Attach each side piece to the fabric that covers the top of the table. You now have a tent that covers the top of the table and hangs to the floor on all 4 sides. Mark and stitch or bind doors and windows in side pieces. It's easiest to add details to sides and roof at this point. See photo above.

Make shutters, doors, flowers and shrubs by appliqué. Or use fabric crayons or liquid embroidery pens to paint on features. Children can help color these parts of the house. To add challenge, combine teaching activities with the house. Add zipper for doorway and fix window shutters so they tie or snap shut. Let children place flowers and stems on house by making them button, snap or fasten with Velcro. Turn up 1/4-inch hem and stitch.

This card-table house will provide hours of fun for children. And you can fold it up and put it away until next time.

COSTUMES FOR KIDS

Whether your child needs a costume for Halloween, a skit or just for play, these ideas will help you make it quickly and inexpensively.

PAPER SUGAR-BAG COSTUMES

Make a basic costume by cutting slits for head and arms in empty, multi-layer, heavy paper bags used to hold 25, 50 or 100 pounds of sugar. Strip off first layer of paper to reveal plain paper underneath. This can be decorated easily to form basic tunic. Decorate tunic in many ways.

Skeleton—Paint black. Wear with black turtleneck and tights or slacks. Make bones by cutting and pasting on strips of white iron-on tape. Set tape in place with warm iron.

Soldier Or Prince—Paint blue. Wear wide red sash and make cardboard sword to wear at waist. Paste on medals and decorations made from stationery stickers.

Space Traveler—Decorate bag with foil or silver paint. Cut face-hole in box that fits over child's head. Cover box with foil or paint. For important space dials, attach smaller box to front of costume. Paint or attach dials to this box. Use white or silver clothes-dryer vent hose for sleeves. Run small plastic tube for air from back of face box to oxygen tank attached to back of costume.

Adapt sugar-bag costumes for other characters such as Santa Claus, jack-o-lantern, Robin Hood or snowman.

DRAWSTRING COSTUMES

Make costumes from sheets or a large piece of cloth. Cut cloth in long strip. It should measure twice the child's height from shoulder to knees. Width should match child's measurements from elbow to elbow.

Sew casings on top and bottom of material. With right sides together, sew center back seam, leaving casing open. Put elastic through casings, leaving ends protruding. Try sack on child. Mark armholes. Cut slits in side of bag for arms. Turn raw edges in and sew around armhole slits.

Have child step into bag. Pull drawstrings. Stuff with wadded-up newspaper until costume is round and full. Pull drawstring to secure over child's shoulders. Tie. Complete as suggested on next page.

Bubblebath—Blow up 30 pink, white or light-blue round balloons. Tie knot at end. Just before leaving for party, attach tip of balloons with safety pins to jogging suit or leotards and tights. Inflate 2 or 3 balloons with helium if available and attach to back of collar with 2- to 3-foot lengths of string. Child looks like walking bubblebath.

Jar Of Jelly Beans—A heavy, clear plastic drawstring costume may be stuffed with inflated balloons of various colors, making jar of jelly beans.

Jack-O-Lantern—Make jack-o-lantern face on front of sack. Add orange floppy hat with green leaves and stem on top. Have child wear black stockings. Makes child a walking jack-o-lantern.

Pumpkin Or Tomato—Make sack out of orange or red fabric. Cut leaf shapes from green crepe paper and paste in layers, shaped as collar.

Mouse Or Other Animal—Dye sheet or sack appropriate color. Make tail from braided rug yarn or ribbon. Sew tail to back of costume. Do not stuff costume too much. Make animal mask by cutting face-holes in paper plate and decorating with features. Make a single hole on each side of mask and attach strings or elastic to tie mask to child's head. Use construction paper half-circles or cones to form muzzles or noses. Decorate with yarn mane and hair. Use pipe cleaners for whiskers.

Google Eyes from Egg Carton

Wig

Beard and Moustache

SIMPLE COSTUME ACCESSORIES

These simple accessories provide finishing touches to costumes.

Moustache—Fold 2x6" or 2x8" piece of brown paper bag in half. Draw half of moustache along fold. Cut and open. Tape to upper lip. Fringe and curl bottom of moustache.

Glasses Or Google Eyes—Cut two adjoining individual sections from egg carton. Cut eye holes at bottom of each section. Cut small half-circle away from between sections so glasses fit over nose. Punch holes on each side of glasses. Reinforce holes with tape. Attach string or piece of elastic through reinforced hole to tie on glasses. Loop over ears or tie at back of head. Decorate with marking pens to make funny glasses or silly google eyes.

Paper-Bag Hair—Choose flat-bottomed paper bag large enough to fit over child's head. Cut away most of front section. For bangs around face, leave 4 to 6 inches at top of bag and 2 to 3 inches on each side. Fringe bottom and side edges of bag by slitting bag every 1/4 to 3/4 inch. Wind each fringed section around pencil for a few minutes to curl hair.

Beard—Cut medium-size paper bag to about 9x12" rectangle. Longest side should reach from nose to end of desired beard. Fringe bottom for beard. Cut small opening for mouth. Fringe top edges for moustache. Roll fringes around pencil to make curly. Reinforce each side of beard at top with a small piece of tape. Pull string or elastic through holes to loop over ears or tie at back of head.

YOUNG VISITORS' ENTERTAINMENT KIT

This kit is made for little friends who come with their parents to visit. You may enjoy visiting with the adults, but you have nothing for little ones to play with. By planning ahead and creating your own entertainment kit, children enjoy their visit. And your home won't turn into a disaster area.

Bookmark Surprises—Encourage quiet play indoors by filling a plastic dishpan with books, crayons and already cut-out animal bookmarks. Children color their own markers. They can use them while reading books. Marker makes a nice surprise to take home.

Quart-Size Milk-Carton Bowling—Save 1-quart milk or orange-juice cartons. Rinse thoroughly, dry and tape openings shut. Purchase a rubber or sponge ball for bowling and set up 10 milk-carton pins at end of an alley or bowling space you make in a secluded room. Your quiet indoor bowling game is complete.

Unbirthday Drawer—Pick up 25¢ to 50¢ odds-and-ends while shopping. Put in your unbirthday drawer. When children come to visit, let them select an unbirthday gift to play with and take home.

Hobby Boxes—To keep children occupied, have these handy hobby boxes on hand. Label and fill several shoe boxes with such supplies as:

Rock People. Box might contain smooth and odd-shaped rocks, paints, brushes and glue. Let children make rock people.

Play Jewelery. Box can include colored macaroni, old jewelry, cut-up drinking straws and string.

Picture Letters. Box might include old magazines, paper, scissors and glue to illustrate a letter or story.

Brown-Paper Sack Puppets. Box might contain brown lunch-size paper bags, yarn, string, scraps of felt and magic markers to make puppets.

Tom and Dian make Photo Under Glass and Mounted Cut-Out photo displays.

Families

8

GOOD FAMILY RELATIONSHIPS

A challenge in any family is to maintain happy, loving relationships. Use your imagination to create thoughtful gifts or messages that tell loved ones you do *not* take them for granted.

KINDNESS FOR YOUR SPOUSE

What's more important than making your relationship with your spouse the best possible? These ideas will help even during busiest times.

Prepare A Timed Message—Hook up a cassette recorder to a turn-on timer. Set time to go off when spouse is at home. The tape will deliver a special "I love you" message of appreciation and warmth.

Weekly Date—A weekly time together can renew a relationship. A show, dinner, even a walk, provides time to share adult experiences. If you can't spare an evening, meet for lunch between appointments and obligations. It's amazing what a weekly get-away can do for both of you.

Help Each Other—Experts save time. Let each person choose household tasks, then research how to do them best. One might learn how to wallpaper well, while another learns about painting or carpet laying. Two experts on the same subject often mean time wasted in disagreements. Instead, let one organize a task and one support it to help each other.

KINDNESS TO CHILDREN, GRANDCHILDREN OR YOUNG FRIENDS

Children need all the love and attention they can get. Try these tips to let them know you care.

Save-The-Day Time—Create a 20-minute, save-the-day time. As you walk in the door after work, all the problems of the day come rushing at you from children and spouse. Stop fighting and flow with it. Sit down, take off your shoes and give yourself 20 minutes with your family. Dinner can wait.

Memories In Concrete—Permanent memories in concrete make good garden stepping stones. You'll need disposable foil pans, a large bag of pre-mixed concrete (all you add is water), a board or metal spatula and an eager child.

Choose foil pans of suitable size for stepping stones. Turkey roaster pans, 16-3/4x12x3-1/2'', make ideal molds. Following directions for the concrete, mix enough to cover bottom of pan to depth of 2 to 3 inches. Pour concrete into pan. Use a board on its side or metal spatula to even out concrete and smooth the surface.

Cover child's hands with petroleum jelly. Then have him press his hands in concrete. Have him sign his name or scratch in a picture with a stick. Whatever masterpiece your child creates, you'll want to identify the work with his name and the date. When concrete sets, turn pan over and block will pop out.

Use stepping stones in backyard or garden to preserve child's handiwork. You'll be amazed how often children will place their hands over the imprints to measure their growth.

Lollipop Garden—Before young children come for a visit, plant a lollipop garden. Put lollipop sticks down in a dirt flowerbed or planter box so they look like growing flowers. Children will enjoy picking these sweet flower treats.

Nutritious Snacks—When your children return home from school, try these easy, nutritious snacks they can fix and munch on.

- Vegetables the children helped prepare the night before, with dip.
- Flour tortillas topped with shredded cheese and popped in the microwave. For an added treat, spread tortilla with spaghetti sauce or pizza topping before adding cheese. Roll up and eat.
- Fruit yogurt and granola they can mix together.

Their Own Books—Convert inexpensive photo albums into personalized books to record experiences with a particular child or grandchild. Paste in the snapshots, mementos, postcards of places you've been or magazine pictures of activities. Write a few words about memories you've shared. Children will enjoy reading their own personal memory book.

Show What You Expect—Write or draw household rules and chores on card or posterboard. Post in prominent place or on family bulletin board. Take time to go through rules and chores with each child individually. Let child know exactly what you expect.

Praise And Recognition—Create awards, certificates, special privileges, words of praise and recognition. Present them for jobs well done, peacemaking or getting along under difficult circumstances. Recognition and praise, when deserved, go a long way with children.

A Special Birthday Gift—When a child is born, save the newspaper printed on that day. It is a special present for a 21st birthday. Not only the news, but fashions and prices will be novel and interesting to the grownup child.

Variation: Mark a large manilla envelope with child's name when he is born. Slip in birthday newspaper, letters, cards, artwork and other special mementos throughout child's growing years.

School And You—At the beginning of each school year, contact children's teachers. Let them know of your support and concern. Give them your telephone number and other emergency numbers. Ask them to keep you informed of difficulties and give you suggestions on ways to help your child.

Frozen Cookie Batches—Mix a large batch of favorite cookies. Choose cookie dough that freezes well. Roll dough into tube shape and freeze small portion with baking instructions taped on outside of freezer wrap. This keeps older kids happy and busy on a boring afternoon.

Just-For-You Box—For a child who visits regularly, cover a shoebox with colorful contact paper. Label box with child's name. Gather treasures such as an interesting rock, a cocoon and other objects and toys. When child comes to visit, he will appreciate "just-for-you" treasures in his own special box.

Grandparent's Picture Letter—When you write to young grandchildren who can't read, add hand-drawn pictures. The letter will be special for children who are eager to receive mail. They can be valued memories if letters are tucked away in their treasure box.

Grandparent's Pocket Change—It's not always easy to buy a gift for a child's birthday or special occasion. Some grandparents solve this problem by giving money. Make giving money fun by going to each gift-giving event with a pocketful or bag of change. The child receiving the gift reaches into a pocket or bag filled with change. All the money the child can hold in one hand is his to keep.

A Puzzle Letter—When you write to a child, glue the letter on cardboard and cut into a jigsaw puzzle. Send the pieces. Child will enjoy putting puzzle together to read the letter.

Walking Duck—This duck will entertain young children for hours. You'll need:

1 12x18x1-inch pine board
1 old automobile tire inner-tube
30" of a 7/16-inch dowel
4" of a 1-inch dowel
Paint of various colors
White glue

Using the pattern at right as a guide, draw the duck's body on the pine board. Use a compass to draw wheels on the board approximately 3 inches in diameter. Cut parts out with a jigsaw or sabre saw. Sand and paint.

Cut off 3 inches from the end of the 7/16-inch dowel. This becomes the axle for the wheels. Drill a 7/16-inch hole through the center of the wheels. Attach the axle dowel through one wheel, the duck and the other wheel.

Next, attach the shaft. Bore a 7/16-inch hole into the top of the duck's back at a 45-degree angle. Insert the 27" length of dowel into the hole. Drill a 7/16-inch hole into the center of the 1-inch dowel. Fit this handle on the shaft.

Cut wings and feet from the inner-tube using the pattern. Attach wings to the body by sliding them into openings cut 3/4-inch below center of back as shown in the pattern. Attach feet by making a 3/4-inch cut in the sides of each wheel. Insert the foot and glue.

DISPLAY FAVORITE PHOTOS

Try one of the following ideas for an unusual way to display your favorite photographs.

Photo Under Glass—Display photographs in glass jars with granny-cap tops. Put 1 picture in each jar. A 5x7 photo fits perfectly in a quart jar. Gallon jars hold 8x10 photos. Clear glass jars without writing work best.

Make an attractive granny cap for your photo jar. You'll need a 12-inch square of fabric, cotton balls or quilt batting, enough narrow elastic to fit snugly around the neck of the jar and one yard each of lace, seam binding and narrow ribbon.

Cut a circle from the cloth. Cut a 10-inch diameter for a gallon jar, a 9-inch diameter for a wide-mouth quart jar and a 7-inch diameter for a regular-size quart jar. Turn the edge under and sew lace around the outside of the circle. On the wrong side of the fabric draw a circle on the fabric where the elastic will be placed. While pulling elastic tight, sew it on the cap with a zigzag stitch.

Turn cap to right side and fill with cotton balls or quilt batting. Place on jar and tie ribbon around gathered part to complete decoration. See photo and illustration.

Photo Under Glass

Walking Duck

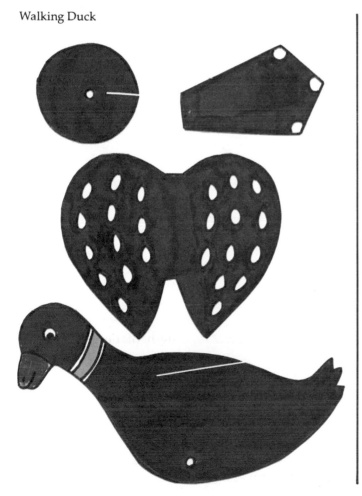

School Days Photo Display—Trace your child's growing years by mounting school photos together. Carefully cut out child's head from photo. Place photos side by side, as in the picture above. Find a rectangular frame to fit photos. If child is beginning school, purchase a frame and add a new photo each year.

If you have only a small photo, have it enlarged and then mount it. It's fun to see the changes from year to year.

Mounted Cut-Out—Make a clever decoration from a large snapshot or studio portrait. Take a favorite photo to a poster shop and have it enlarged. Carefully paste photo figure on a 1/8-inch sheet of polystyrene, available at art stores.

Using a knife or single-edge razor blade, cut out figure or figures you want to display. Cut 2 triangular pieces of polystyrene and attach to back of photo. Figure will stand by itself.

HELP FOR PARENTS

Children can be sweet and loveable. But as every parent will admit, they can often cause irritation and anger. Family rules could ease you over the rough spots of family life. Here are a few suggestions to help smooth wrinkles in your family's relationships.

Time Out—When children are on edge, tense, angry or pressured, call "Time Out!" Everyone goes to a predetermined chair, bed or room to stay until a set amount of cooling-down time elapses.

School Skills Support—If your child has trouble with reading, writing, spelling or arithmetic, hire him to do work for you to practice that skill. For instance, a child with poor arithmetic skills can learn to add and subtract with greater ease by helping figure the family budget. He can add up the grocery bill or balance the checkbook. A child having trouble reading can help go through mail, magazines and other reading material to find specific information. A child with writing or spelling problems can serve as secretary, writing letters dictated by family members.

Curfew Alarm—Use an alarm clock to help teenagers come home on time. Teenagers and parents set the alarm for the time teen is to return. Teenager must get home in time to turn off alarm so parents do not waken. If the alarm goes off before the teenager has returned, he must pay the agreed-upon consequences.

Reward Good Behavior—On a day when children have refrained from quarreling, let them reach into a special grab bag for a small toy, treat or special privilege.

Red-Letter Day—Honor a birthday person or child receiving a good grade at school with a special placesetting at dinner. Purchase one placesetting of a special color or design. Use it as the Place of Honor for a reward.

PRESERVING MEMORIES

Many of us enjoy nostalgia. Turning the pages of an old yearbook, rummaging in a box of childhood treasures, reading an old diary, talking with a friend, looking into the past—all bring back pleasant memories.

It's easy to misplace mementos and lose important treasures from the past. The following tips can help you preserve special memories, treasures and traditions.

WAYS TO SAVE MEMORIES

Memories are important to you and your family. The following ideas will help save your memories so they can be enjoyed for a long time.

Memory Quilts—When your child wears out a favorite pair of pants, skirt, shirt, blouse or dress, don't just put it in the ragbag. Find an unworn piece or pieces and snip them out. Place them in a box marked with child's name. If you sew, save scraps from garments you make your children in similar boxes.

When you collect enough scraps, sew them into a quilt top. A memory quilt makes a perfect gift when child goes away to college, takes a new job or marries.

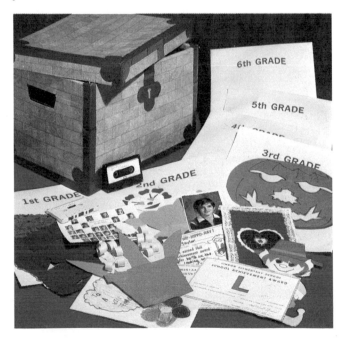

Shadow Box Memories—Whether you're looking for a special gift to commemorate an occasion or a way to preserve treasured mementos, a shadow box can provide a reminder of special times. You can purchase a shadow box at a craft or hobby store. Or make one yourself with wood backing and wooden yardstick strips for edging and box sections.

Arrange photographs, wedding announcements or special items such as keys and corsages in box. Use miniatures purchased at craft and hobby stores. Miniature typewriters, books, tennis racquets and pots and pans symbolize hobbies, careers and areas of interest.

Organize and secure items to box with glue. Find a special spot to hang your shadow box.

Treasure Box—Need a place for report cards, snapshots, dance programs, pressed flowers, class pictures and business certificates? If so, you'll appreciate this treasure box.

Choose a box of adequate size and sturdiness. A cardboard file box is ideal. Cover with colorful contact paper or decorate to your taste. Put personal treasures in it for safekeeping.

If particularly well organized, you may want a second treasure box to file treasures in folders or envelopes arranged in chronological order. Make one for preschool, grade school and so on. At the end of each school year or on birthdays, sit down with child and let him choose school papers, drawings, snapshots or mementos he wants to keep.

Heritage Box—A heritage box is similar to a treasure box. Make photocopies of ancestors' pictures. Cut and paste into a collage on the side of the box. Use a map of the locales and countries of ancestors to decorate one side of box. Construct a family tree for top, arranging pictures of immediate ancestors with their parents and grandparents on branches of the tree. Your picture is on trunk of tree.

To preserve priceless photos, place each photo in a special tissue envelope that you can buy in most photography stores. Pictures and mementos of the countries of your ancestors' births, letters and accounts of their lives and oral histories of living ancestors recorded on tape will be priceless to you and your descendants.

DOCUMENTING MEMORIES

It's important to write down your memories to preserve them. But it's not easy to do. Here are some ways to help you preserve memories without expending too much energy.

Writing Your History—Writing memoirs isn't just for famous people. Anyone can do it. It's hard to find time to write down or record your own life story, but here's an easy method. If you correspond fairly regularly, slip an extra piece of paper and carbon paper under stationery when you write. Keep carbon copies in a special file or memory box for hours of nostalgia, laughter and tears in years to come.

Short-Term Scrapbooks—Writing about family activities and pasting a year's worth of snapshots into a picture album seems overwhelming. Why not preserve short spans of time—a summer, a special event or a particular vacation?

Before the event, buy an inexpensive photo album with about 10 pages. On the first sheet, write event or time period covered: Summer of 1985 or Our 25th Wedding Anniversary. As days pass and mementos and pictures accumulate, slip them into the books. By the end of the year, your books will be full of recorded memories.

Handy Tip: Place each picture's negative under corresponding picture in your photo albums.

FAMILY-REUNION MEMORIES

You can make your family reunion more exciting. It doesn't matter whether the reunion is an informal gathering of the immediate family, a yearly assembling of grandparents' progeny or a formal reunion of people descended from a common great-grandparent.

With a little imagination, planning and a few simple suggestions, you can promote fun and family pride. You'll want to adapt these activities and tips to the size and needs of your family group.

MEMENTOS

Mementos can draw your family together. They can be special gifts to present to a particular honored relative or some token for everyone to take home.

Photo Family-Identifiers—Choose a family portrait, a picture of a common ancestor or a symbol of your family. Add fancy-lettered family motto or family name. Have picture and lettering transferred to tee-shirts, tote bags, calendars, colorful caps or other items. Each person attending can take item home as a reminder of the reunion.

Family Quilt—Make a family quilt as a stitched memory for a parent, grandparent or other relative. Every person or family unit contributes a quilt block, then blocks are joined.

If you use fabric crayons, young and old and even those who do not embroider can participate. Each person draws his idea on a sheet of typing paper and signs his name and age. Letters and numbers must be written backward so when held up in a mirror, they read correctly. Children may draw a special symbol or a pretty picture.

Next, place drawing or design face down on quilt block. A square or rectangle of muslin or other lightweight, heat-resistant fabric works well. Secure drawing and block so they will not slip. Iron, following directions on fabric crayon package. Design will transfer permanently to fabric.

Each quilt block reflects donor's tastes, talent and age. The quilt preserves a family memory by capturing each contributor's personality. It is a decorative, lasting family memory.

FAMILY-REUNION ACTIVITIES

Use the following suggestions to spark your creativity. Your family can adapt, change and create activities suited to your group.

Come As You Were—Each family member comes dressed in a costume or carrying special props that stand for a particular person or event from his past. For example, Grandfather might come dressed in a uniform. Grandmother might wear her college graduation cap and gown. Each person stands and tells the story of the particular achievement or event he is dressed like.

Variation: Dress as an ancestor or family member you admire. Everyone comes prepared to tell about the person he is dressed like.

This-Is-Your-Life Drama Bags—If centering your reunion around a particular family member or ancestor, a version of *This Is Your Life* lets everyone participate in and enjoy the event.

Divide family into groups of equal number. Hand each group a card with the outline of a different event important in the life of the honored ancestor or family member. Give each group a bag of props appropriate to the event. Each must dramatize its event, using props or anything else they can come up with.

Allow the group members time to organize and cast their presentation. Dramatizations are presented in the order in which they happened. Fill in gaps with narration so program presents an imaginative, informative picture of the person's life. Record it for posterity.

Gathering The Group—One tip many reunion organizers have found helpful. It may be hard to gather everyone together or get everyone's attention. It's equally difficult to call them in from activities to accomplish the business of the reunion. Use a bullhorn, boat horn, whistle or other noise-maker. It signals the end of individual activities and the beginning of group business.

Family Olympics—Hold your own Olympics. Have family members of all ages compete for gold, silver or bronze medals. Here's a sample of some of the events you may want to run.

Olympic Torch—Use ingenuity in creating Olympic competition. One family used a charcoal hibachi and had a runner jog in with a torch at beginning of the competition to light their "Olympic flame."

Double Dash—Grandparent and grandchild are teamed together for this race. Tie left leg of one partner to right leg of other. Partners learn teamwork to match strides and beat other teams.

Javelin Throw—Each participant blows the paper covering from a straw as far as he can, using classic Olympic form, of course. Person blowing cover the farthest wins. If paper-covered straws are not available, throw the straw. Person who throws the straw farthest wins.

Shot-Put—Participants try to throw paper plate or Frisbee into washtub or container 10 to 15 feet away. Each participant has three tries and is scored points for each successful try.

Marksmanship—Let five lighted candles provide targets for would-be marksmen armed with water pistols. Stand 3 to 4 feet from candles and try to squirt them out.

Races—Vary 50- and 100-meter dashes by making up challenging races. In one race, have contestants blow cotton balls across piece of plastic. In another, have contestants race, carrying cotton ball, balloon or egg in a spoon. If you drop your load, you must start over.

Ribbons And Awards—Award medals to winners of each event. Purchase medallions at trophy stores. Attach them to lengths of striped red, white and blue ribbon. Give points to winners of first, second and third places. Award medals to those who make the most points.

Taped Anthems—Present awards in true Olympic-style ceremonies complete with songs. Have each family branch choose its own anthem. Award prizes for first, second and third places at special ceremonies during which anthem is sung by group.

Dian explains to Bryant Gumbel how to delegate family responsibilities.

It's About Time

Secretaries, corporate presidents, parents, teenagers—everyone can use more time. Why not spend less time on things you don't like to do and more time on recreation, relaxation or other activities you enjoy?

This section presents techniques and tips to help you save time on day-to-day tasks. Choose one or all of these techniques for planning time, color-coding your household, delegating responsibilities and organizing your home. They can add extra hours and extra energy to your day.

TIME SAVERS

Organizing yourself and your activities is time well invested. Adapting the following simple techniques to your special needs can help you toward a more satisfying use of time.

Setting Goals And Priorities—Goals are important to you. The first step to efficient use of time is to write out long-term and short-term goals. Review your list regularly to make sure day-to-day activities move you toward your goals.

Day-To-Day Planning—Break goals into realizable or achievable day-to-day activities. Then schedule and prioritize.

Time-Saving Tips—Try these time-saving tips to help you make your life more orderly.

- Have an extra set of keys. Keep extra house and car keys in your wallet or other accessible place. If you lock yourself out, you'll be able to save time and trouble by using your spare keys.
- Speed up correspondence. If appropriate, answer correspondence right on the letter when you receive it. When you want an immediate response from someone, enclose a self-addressed, stamped envelope in your letter. If it's a business letter, be sure to make a photocopy and keep it.
- Get rid of extra paper. Almost ninety percent of the paper in your home or office is never referred to again. Get rid of as much of it as possible.
- Keep tools in work center. Leave easy-to-misplace, often-used tools in work centers where you use them most. For instance, place a pen and paper near the telephone. Keep scissors in a convenient drawer but out of reach of children.

- Have a secret shelf for gifts. When you find something on sale or have time to shop, buy gifts in quantity. Wrap and tag them for future giving.
- Buy birthday and anniversary cards for the whole year in January. Sign and address them. Label the stamp corner of each card with the date to be mailed. Store them in your tickler file (see below) or a box near your calendar. Check your file each week and mail when necessary.
- Prepare double. When you cook, prepare double the amount you require for one meal. Freeze the rest to use for future meals. Make up revolving menus. Write one week's menus on the right side of your Shopping List, as described on page 152. Make menu sheets for 7 to 10 weeks, then alternate them throughout the year.
- Prepare clothing in advance. Set aside clothes the night before you wear them. Check for spots to be cleaned, needed repairs or pressing before you put clothes on.

To-Do List—Write down all of the tasks, appointments, chores and errands you need to accomplish each day. Use the tickler file described below to help you keep track of what you must do. Take time to prioritize items on your list. Rank each item as follows: A for the most important items; B for items you should do next; and C for items you can afford to neglect. You may want to prioritize even further, ranking A items 1, 2, 3 in order of importance.

Work at each task according to its ranking, completing the most important first (A-1). Cross off each task as you complete it.

Tickler File—When paperwork starts mounting, start a tickler file. Purchase a cardboard file box. Make a file for each month. In addition, make a file for each day of the month. Then organize your life. As papers, appointments and deadlines come in, file them in their appropriate monthly file. Events several months ahead are filed by month initially. At the beginning of that month papers are filed under the appropriate day, using the daily files from last month's folders. Each morning pull out the day's file and organize your day. You can program your household chores on daily, weekly and monthly cards. Drop them in the files to keep ahead of your responsibilities.

COLOR-CODING

An easy way to organize your household is by color-coding. Each person chooses a different color for his belongings such as drinking cup, toothbrush, towel and washcloth. Color-coding prevents confusion and keeps items organized and ready to use.

Color-Coded Clothing—Color-coding can help you identify look-alike clothing. Sew a few stitches of colored thread to waists of shorts, pantyhose, tee-shirts and other clothing. Use family member's color to identify garments. Colored threads make laundry sorting quicker and easier. Or label garments with dot of permanent laundry marker in appropriate color.

Color-Coded Linens—Color-code bed linens by size. Purchase all single-bed sheets, blankets and matching pillowcases in shades and prints of the same color. All double-bed sheets are another color. Fold sets together. Color-coding by size allows family members to find bed linens almost instantly.

Color-Coded Clothes Hangers—To avoid confusion when two family members share a closet, mark hanger tops with strips of tape in appropriate colors. Or hang clothes belonging to each person on hangers of his color. Even young children can locate clothing quickly this way.

Color-Coded Laundry Management—To help simplify washing, try this system. Provide one laundry basket for each individual. Purchase basket in person's color or label with tape or paint. As you fold, iron or pick up articles, place them in correct laundry basket. It's easier for each person to put away clean laundry.

Another system of color-coded laundry hampers or baskets helps family members sort clothes for washing. Use three baskets or hampers large enough to hold one washerload each. Buy white for all-white clothes, medium color for light-colored clothes and dark color for dark-colored clothes. Family members put dirty clothes, towels and other items into appropriate baskets or hampers. Saves time sorting mixed clothes.

Color-Coded Calendar—A color-coded appointment calendar helps keep telephone messages and appointments straight.

Materials needed:
- An appointment calendar the size of a large desk calendar.
- Posterboard larger than calendar.
- 6x11'' felt pieces in different color for each family member.
- Fine-tipped marking pens to match felt colors.
- Heavy-duty glue.
- Decorations for each family member's pocket.

To assemble:
1. Glue calendar to posterboard leaving 6-inch strip below calendar.
2. Fold up 4-1/2 inches on each 6x11'' piece of felt to form pocket.
3. Stitch each side of pocket.
4. For marking pens, stitch another vertical seam 1 inch from left side of pocket.
5. Glue color-coded pockets on posterboard.
6. Decorate felt pockets and backstrip with family pictures, pompons, names or characters.
7. Mount calendar conveniently near telephone and scratch pad.

To use:
Record appointments, dates and special events with marking pen in person's color on calendar. Everyone can see schedule for Monday after school or whether car will be busy Friday night. Telephone messages and daily task assignments can be placed in individual's felt pocket.

Color-Coded Phone-And-Address Book—Try organizing your address book with colored dots. Dot school addresses in red, business acquaintances in green, personal friends in yellow, service personnel (hairdresser, seamstress, plumber) in blue. When you look at a page, you can pick out friends' numbers without reading through each name on the page. This also helps when sending Christmas cards. Color-code list showing to whom you sent or from whom you received Christmas cards. When using card file, use different color card for categories.

Color-Code Important Papers And Files—A strip of colored adhesive across tops of file folders can help you file and find important household papers at a glance.

**Blue Files for
Insurance Papers**
Life policies
Health policies
Auto policies
House policies

**Green Files for
Employment Records**
Social Security
Pension information
Past employers
Dates and references
Resumés

**Yellow Files for
Financial Information**
Checking accounts
Savings accounts
Loan contracts
Mortgage numbers and
contracts
Credit card numbers
Investment records

**Pink Files for
Household Inventory**
List for each room
Photos of possessions

**White Files for
Personal Certificates**
Birth certificates
Marriage records
Wills

**Orange Files for
Health Records**
Immunization records
Disease records

**Brown Files for
School Records**
Certificates
Report cards
Diplomas

**Purple Files for
Guarantees**
Service guarantees
Appliance warranties

**Red Files for
Tax Records**
Income sources
Contributions
Interest paid
Medical and dental expenses
Deductible taxes
Childcare expenses
Casualty losses
Union and professional dues

DELEGATING HOUSEHOLD RESPONSIBILITIES

Need some help in delegating household tasks and motivating family members to finish them? Here are some great ideas.

CHILDREN AND HOUSEHOLD CHORES

Children need help and encouragement with household chores. These ideas will help them get through chores and maybe even like doing them.

Give House A Birthday Party—Assign everyone a deep-cleaning job such as washing walls, cleaning closets or cleaning drapes. When tasks are completed, have a party complete with cake and ice cream.

Housework Modeling—Help children learn to do a task thoroughly by working with them the first few times they do it. A parent, older sister or brother can guide child the first few times he cleans his room, sets the table or cleans the sink. This "buddy system" creates a model and helps establish good work habits.

Mr. Duster—Make dusting fun for younger children by attaching face of felt pieces on end of clean, absorbent sock or homemade duster. Commercial car washing mitt does very well. Children can slip Mr. Duster over hand and help him gobble up dirt.

What Children Should Know—Young children should know vital information such as:
- Full name
- Parents' full names
- Grandparents' names
- Phone number
- Birthdate
- Parents' work numbers
- Whom to call in case of emergency (grandparent, sitter, neighbor)
- How to lock and unlock the house
- Other information as it applies to your family

When the child has learned everything on your "information list," he is rewarded by a date with a parent, a long-distance call to a relative or friend, or an overnight stay with grandparents.

3x5 Dinner Planner—Create a file card for each of your 30 favorite dinner menus. Many entrees have standard salads and drinks. As an example, with spaghetti you often serve a green salad and garlic bread. On one side of a 3x5 card list main dish, vegetables, salad, drink and dessert. On the opposite side list all items needed for menu. When planning a week's menu, select 7 cards and make your shopping list from items on the cards. Then post cards on your refrigerator door. The first one home can begin dinner.

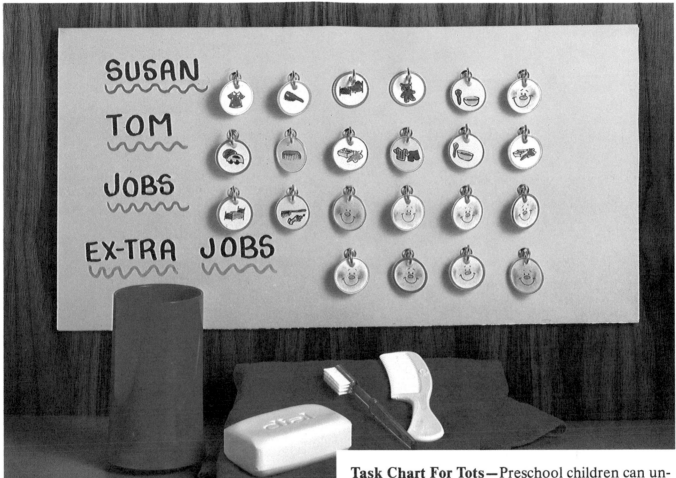

Task Chart For Tots—Preschool children can understand simple line charts with the name of a task and picture to remind child what to do. Bed-making line on chart might show picture of a bed. Cleaning-up-the-bedroom line might show picture of room with toys placed neatly on shelves. Draw series of empty squares after each picture. As child completes tasks, put foil star or colorful sticker in corresponding square.

Another method is to make a permanent chart with children's names, jobs and a line of hooks on a board. On each hook hang disk with picture of tasks to be accomplished. As child completes task, turn disk over to reveal smiling face on other side.

Cupcake Delegation—A novel way to assign household chores is to bake assignments into cupcakes or muffins. Write tasks on small slips of paper. Roll or fold papers in foil and place in bottom of cupcake liners in muffin tin. Fill liners with cupcake batter and bake. As you hand out cupcakes, you're delegating weekly chores! Assignments can even be placed in cupcake after baking.

Variation: Place papers in bottom of flat ice-cream cones. Fill cones 2/3 full with cake batter. Place on baking sheet and bake.

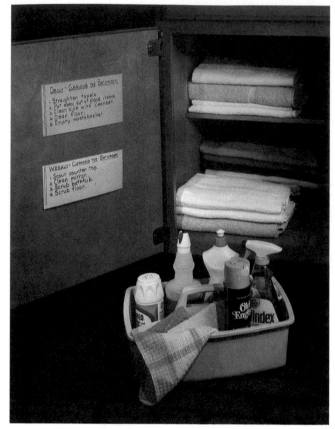

Task Placemats—To simplify mealtime tasks, label placemats with task to perform. One placemat may bear the label "telephone." Person sitting at that place would answer phone during dinner. Another placemat may be labeled "refrigerator." Person at that spot would get items from the refrigerator needed during the meal.

Another way to assign chores is to write tasks on cards. Slip card face down under each drinking glass.

Reward For Cleaning—Encourage thorough cleaning by providing surprise rewards. Place markers or tokens under, on or around items to be dusted. You'll provide incentive for family members to clean thoroughly because they get to turn in their markers to Mom or Dad for cash or favors. You'll also be able to judge quality of cleaning job by number of markers remaining after job is finished.

Weekly Meal Assignments—When a child is old enough to work in the kitchen, assign him one meal a week to plan, prepare and clean up. Have him turn in a menu plan the Saturday before. This gives parents the opportunity to work with the child to teach good nutrition, cooking techniques and efficient clean-up.

Cleaning Cards—Spell out step by step exactly what each job includes. Write steps on card. Cover with clear contact paper or laminate with plastic. Make separate card for daily tidying steps and weekly deep-cleaning steps. Put cards inside closet or cabinet door. For instance, card for daily tidying of bathroom might include:
1. Straighten towels and washcloths.
2. Put away out-of-place clothes and cosmetics.
3. Clean sink and tub with cleanser.
4. Clean mirror.
5. Shake rug.

Card for weekly cleaning might add:
1. Polish countertop.
2. Clean mirror.
3. Scour bathtub, tile walls and fixtures.
4. Wipe floor with disinfectant.
5. Clean toilet.
6. Change towels.
7. Straighten drawers and cupboards.

Early Bird Gets The Easiest Chore—To get family up and going, list chores for the day or a special dinner on a blackboard. Assignments are chosen on first-come, first-choice basis by each family member. For those who fail to follow through and complete their tasks, it's cleanup and dish duty.

Barrel Of Necessities—On one of your quick trips through the house, put all items left out of place in a barrel or plastic garbage can. It is the responsibility of owners to look in barrel and put away their own items.

Money Jobs—To teach children to work and provide extra money, designate *regular jobs* and *money jobs* around the house. Regular jobs are chores they do on a regular basis such as cleaning their room, making beds, doing dishes and cleaning the bathroom.

Money jobs provide extra monetary rewards. Pay children for jobs such as washing the car, cleaning out the garage and washing windows. Pay a reasonable price for each job so they realize they're helping the family and earning money for themselves. Post a list so children can choose jobs as money is needed.

Quality of the job is important. Payment is received after finished job passes inspection. Touch-ups may be required. This helps children learn to do a good job.

Delegating To Teach—Besides keeping the house clean, one reason for household tasks is to teach children skills for independence and adult living. List skills you would like your children to learn before they leave home. Bring children together and assign appropriate tasks to teach skills. Lists can span all age ranges—toddlers, grade-school youth and teenagers. Possible skills you want children to learn may include:

Laundry
Sorting
Operating machines
Using washing aids
Ironing and pressing

Sewing
Mending
Upholstery repair
Basic clothing construction

Cooking
Basic nutrition
Measuring ingredients
Basic techniques such as beating and blending
Egg, meat and vegetable cookery
Baking
Preparing basic casseroles
Using kitchen tools and appliances
Proper cleanup and sanitation

Housekeeping
Dishes
General cleanup
Beds
Dusting
Vacuuming
Scrubbing floors
Bathroom cleaning
Oven cleaning
Refrigerator defrosting and cleaning
Carpet cleaning
Window washing

Shopping
Budgeting and self-control
Coupon buying
Comparison shopping
Recognizing quality
Seasonal buying

Spin-The-Wheel Chart—A wheel chart provides an easy way to assign tasks and make sure everyone gets a turn at easy and hard chores. To make chart, cut small circle and large circle from stiff posterboard or cardboard. Mark sections of small circle with individual names. Divide chores and label sections of large circle with tasks. Cover circles with clear contact paper. Fasten circles together in center with a brad to form spinner. Let children take turns spinning the wheel to see which chores they'll do for a week. A good system is to change tasks each week.

Pick-Up Organizers—These save everyone time and energy.
- *5-Minute Pick Up.* Pick up and dust in each room for five minutes. Time yourself with kitchen timer.
- *10 Pick Up.* Each child picks up 10 out-of-place items and races to put them away. First one to complete race gets a reward.
- *Wandering Laundry Basket.* When cleaning or picking up, take a laundry basket to gather out-of-place items. As you clean, take items and put in laundry basket. As you clean from room to room, put away items in correct room.

Encouraging Proper Table Setting—Here's a way to teach children to set the table properly. Buy a plain-colored vinyl placemat for each family member and contact paper to complement kitchen or dining-room colors. Turn plate, glass and flatware upside-down on back of contact paper. Trace silhouette and cut out. Remove backing from contact paper and place silhouettes on placemats in appropriate spots. Children match flatware, plate and glass to corresponding silhouettes to set table perfectly every time.

Points Per Week—To give older children more choice of cleaning tasks, try a points-per-week system. List all cleaning tasks and assign points to each cleaning chore. For example, vacuuming living room and dining room, 15 points; putting out garbage, 5 points; and so on.

Each family member completes designated number of points each week. Jobs and points are posted. Once a week, family members gather to report points and select new jobs. Family member with most points gets to choose jobs first. Each takes turn selecting one job at a time. Adjustments are made on number of points for younger children.

This practice allows older children to select jobs they can work into their schedules. It also frees Mom and Dad from nagging about the job.

EASY REMINDERS

The following ideas will help you know what is going on at your house. Projects are fun to make and will keep family informed about events and activities.

House Rules—Make a construction-paper house for your refrigerator door. On the house list all rules the children are expected to obey. You might want to include:

- Work first, play second.
- Homework before play.
- Home by ____:00.
- Leave a note telling where you are and when you'll return.
- Everyone home by dinnertime.
- Children not getting along must go to their rooms for ____ minutes.
- Study (or practice) a minimum of ____ minutes per night.
- No more than ____ hours of TV per day (more is allowable with permission of parent).
- Leave your work area cleaner and tidier than you found it.
- Unload dishwasher before next meal.
- All children must be washed and dressed by breakfast time.

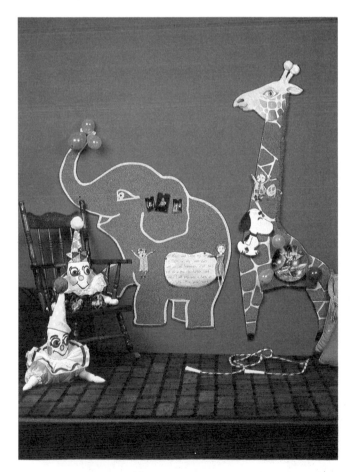

Kitchen Door Bulletin Board—With indoor/outdoor carpet or bulletin board material, cover back of kitchen door or door family uses most often. Attach material to door with carpet glue. This provides a family bulletin board where it is easy to see messages as family members come and go.

Animal Corkboard—An animal shape makes an ideal cork bulletin board. An elephant's round tummy and floppy ears provide plenty of space for attaching notes. Find floppy-eared elephant cartoon in a coloring book and draw a pattern. Or use the photo on the left as a guide. A good pose is circus elephant standing or one sitting back with front legs in the air. Buy corkboard, lightweight 1/8-inch plywood and contrasting 1/2-inch plastic tape.

Cut corkboard and plywood using pattern. Glue together. Outline and trim elephant with plastic tape. Other animals also work well.

ORGANIZING SPACE

Have you ever spent valuable time looking for something you put in a "safe" place so you could find it later? Too much time is wasted hunting for misplaced items. The following tips should make storing, replacing and finding items a matter of seconds rather than minutes or hours.

ORGANIZING STORAGE

It's not easy to organize storage space. Try the following ideas I've gathered to help you use your space wisely.

Limits—Limit amount of each item you store. If you're tempted to keep something in case you might need it, set a limit. For example, if you store newspapers for fireplace tinder, save a stack 2 feet high and no higher.

Self-Sealing Storage Bags—Place items that go together in bags. Use heavy-duty, self-sealing freezer bags. Punch hole in middle of bag below seam. Place toys in bag and display on pegboard. Set up rules so child plays with one bag at a time. Rotate bags from time to time.

Master List Of Seldom-Used Items—Make a master list of storage. List items alphabetically in notebook. Use a page or more for each letter so you can add to list as you add to household.

Plastic Dish Bins—Plastic dish bins make excellent storage places for clothing, toys and other items. To help little ones, tape magazine pictures of contents to outside end of each bin.

Handy Fingerholes In Boxes—If you store clothes and other items in boxes on high shelves, put a fingerhole in front near bottom of box. It's great for sliding box off shelf.

ORGANIZING KITCHEN ITEMS

Most of us spend a lot of time in the kitchen. Having your kitchen organized is one of the best ways to use your time and energy efficiently. Kitchen items are often small and easily misplaced. I've listed some ideas to help you organize things so you can find them easily. These tips will make storage easier and help you save space. With these helpful hints you can enjoy the neatest kitchen on the block!

Simplifying Search For Spices—Cooking time can be cut when you organize spices and condiments in kitchen cupboards or drawers. Arrange spices in alphabetical order. Place pieces of masking tape on containers with consecutive numbers written on them. It's easy to locate what you want in alphabetical sequence. When you're finished, replace spices quickly by number. This is handy for young cooks and helps them keep you organized.

Labeling—Use label-maker or self-sticking labels to mark each section of shelves, drawers, cupboards and closets. If one section of cupboard shelf is marked "dinner plates" and next section is marked "blue tumblers," anyone wiping dishes, unloading the dishwasher or setting the table will know where to find or replace those items.

Carpet-Square Cupboard Cushions—Lay foam-backed carpet squares on bottom of cupboards where you store china and glassware, in flatware drawers or pot-and-pan cupboards. Soft squares reduce breakage and chipping of delicate items. They also prevent items from jostling and slipping around.

Kitchen Savers And Organizers—Use these ideas to save time and energy.

Put a decorative hook by the sink. Hang your watch and rings on it while you work.

Make an "Instruction/Guarantee Manual." Use a looseleaf notebook and divider pages with pockets to arrange and keep together instructions, warranties and guarantees.

Buy a stopwatch. Time yourself and family members when making long-distance phone calls.

Buy a half-cup ice-cream scoop. You'll find one at a restaurant-equipment store. Measure shortening, brown sugar or other ingredients with it. Use a small ice-cream scoop for drop cookies.

Keep track when measuring large quantities. If you're measuring 10 cups, count out as many raisins or chocolate pieces as the number of cups. Eat one after adding each cup.

Recipe Mounting—You'll save time thumbing through recipe drawers, files and cookbooks if you mount favorite or frequently used recipes in accessible places. Here are some common places that have proven handy.

- Purchase Rolodex desk file and type recipes on cards. You can flip to them easily and pages stay open. To keep food from getting spilled on cards, buy plastic covers. Color-code cards for different recipe categories.

- Laminate and mount commonly used recipes inside cupboard door over food preparation area.

- Carefully write recipes with permanent ink on self-stick paper. Put on inside of roll-up window shade over sink. When recipe is needed, pull shade down.

- For artistic chefs who are planning to build or remodel a home, here's an unusual decorator idea. Pick light-colored tiles for kitchen wall around mixing area. Select favorite recipes and have them professionally printed on tiles. They should be fired in a kiln with permanent glaze. When kitchen walls are ready, arrange tiles in area you will use. This will make your kitchen unique and favorite recipes accessible at a glance.

Appliance Cord Storage—Cover cardboard toilet tissue roll with colorful contact paper. Label each roll with name of cord it holds. Roll up appliance cord and slip into roll to keep neat and handy.

Backdoor Organization—Keep your backdoor area organized and your house clean. Hang a rack on the wall for outdoor jackets. Put shelves and bins by the door to hold dirty clothes, toys and sports equipment. Put down a large piece of indoor-outdoor carpeting to absorb mud and water from dirty boots and shoes.

Organizing Flat Pans—Make finding and storing pie pans, baking sheets, cake pans and other items easier by stacking them vertically in dish drainer.

Storing Surplus Canned Goods—Find alternative storage areas other than kitchen cupboards for seldom-used canned goods. A handy place to store cans is in the space under the bed. Make wooden racks that tilt so cans roll to one side of the bed.

Dian and Willard Scott test various household cleaning tips.

Household Hints

Cleaning the house is a chore most people dislike. But it has to be done. There are many ideas in this chapter to help you organize your time to get those cleaning jobs done faster! Tips are provided on the best ways to clean your kitchen, bathroom and other areas of your house.

To many people, shopping is a necessary evil. I've included ideas to help you shop more easily and effectively. A sample Shopping List will help you plan your visits to the supermarket.

HELPFUL HINTS

Try some of the following helpful hints to make life easier.

HANDY IDEAS

Styrofoam Pethouse—For cold winter nights, keep your pet warm by making a pethouse from a Styrofoam ice chest. First glue lid to chest. Invert and cut an entrance at one end, making it large enough for pet to go in and out. With acrylic paints, decorate chest. Styrofoam is a good insulating material and will help keep pet warm during cold winter months.

Mending Kit—Place mending kit with needles, scissors, neutral-colored thread, extra buttons and pins in laundry room. Use it for sewing buttons flicked off in washer or dryer.

Needle In Soap—Punch needle or pin into bar of soap so it will slide through fabric more easily.

Rugged Buttons—Use dental floss as thread to sew on hard-to-hold buttons. Try fine fishing line to sew buttons on coats, mend tents and sew heavy leather or canvas.

Telephone Shutter List—Make your own decorative telephone directory. It's easy and attractive. You'll need:

  1 12'' length of 3/8-inch dowel
  1 wooden movable shutter,
    7-inch-wide or your choice
  Spray varnish
  1 pkg. 2-1/2x1-3/4'' self-adhesive labels

Cut dowel into two equal 6'' lengths. Glue dowels across top and bottom of shutter back. Before gluing top dowel, carve out space in center of dowel for nail to fit into as a hanging point. Varnish shutter.

Type or print phone numbers on labels. Place business labels on closed side of shutter. Open shutter and attach personal numbers to this side. Hang by telephone for easy access.

HINTS FOR GROWING THINGS

Plant A Curtain Rod—"Plant" an adjustable brass curtain rod in pots of tall-growing plants. As plant grows, rod "grows" to provide needed support.

Hoe-Handle Measure—Mark 2-, 4-, 6- and 8-inch rings on handle of hoe or trowel. Use as handy measuring device for spacing seeds, bulbs or rows.

Bulbs—Put non-wintering bulbs you dig up in fall in individual compartments of egg carton. Store them in cool, dry spot until spring. This prevents mildew.

HOT AND COLD PACKS

Help tired or hurt muscles by making a hot or cold pack.

Hot Pack—Soak terry dish towel in warm water. Wrap in plastic wrap. (As shown in photo on left.) Place in microwave oven for a minute or until towel is hot. Wrap in lightweight towel and use as hot pack. For quick relief, use a washcloth instead. Heat cloth in microwave for a few seconds.

Cold Pack—Mix 1 cup water and 1/2 cup rubbing alcohol. Pour mixture into self-sealing plastic bag and freeze. Alcohol will keep mixture slushy so bag will be pliable and fit easily over injured part of body. Keep a couple in freezer for unexpected bumps and bruises.

CLEANING TIPS

These handy, helpful hints can save you valuable minutes—and pennies as well.

IN THE KITCHEN

Try these tips to keep your kitchen sparkling all the time.

Keep Vegetables Fresh And Dry—Line produce and meat drawers in your refrigerator with paper towels. Or slip a clean, dry sponge in the bottom of the drawers to absorb excess moisture.

Baby Oil—Use it to clean a stainless steel sink. Sink will be shiny and clean without water spots.

Citrus Freshener—Put citrus through the disposal to give a clean fresh smell. This is an efficient way to dispose of rinds left after using fruit.

Interruptions When You Work—If the telephone rings when you're working with sticky dough or cleaning something very dirty, dusty or sooty, stick your hand in a plastic bag and answer the phone.

Use Marbles—Keep some marbles in the bottom of your double boiler, vegetable steamer or tea kettle. They'll make all kinds of noise when the water has boiled out.

Use Powder Puff—Use a new, clean powder puff for flouring cake pans.

Common Table Salt (use it straight from the box).
- Clean sticky dough remains from rolling pin and counter surface where you roll out biscuit, pie or cookie dough.
- Clean odor from hands after you've chopped onions.

Baking Soda (use it straight from the box).
- Clean marks off counter tops without scratching the surface.
- Scour burned food from pans.
- Clean and deodorize refrigerator or pet accidents on carpet.
- Put out grease fires by shaking soda on them.

Automatic Dishwasher Detergent (solution of 2 tablespoons per gallon of water).
- Loosen burned or baked-on food from non-cast-iron pans and dishes.
- Remove stains and odors from plastic pitchers and containers.
- Clean plastic sink mats, drain boards, plastic-covered dish drainers.

HOME-MIXED CLEANING SOLUTIONS

Save time and money with these inexpensive, easily made home cleaning solutions. Just be sure you don't mix bleach and ammonia. It gives off a harmful gas.

Heavy-Duty Wall Cleaner—Mix 1 cup ammonia, 1/2 cup vinegar and 1/4 cup baking soda in 1 gallon water. Wash small area of wall. Rinse immediately with clear warm water. Wear rubber gloves when using this cleaner.

General Household Cleaner—Combine 2 tablespoons ammonia and 2 tablespoons liquid detergent in 1 quart water. Use with sponge.

Window-Glass Cleaner—Combine 2 tablespoons non-sudsing ammonia, 1 pint rubbing alcohol and 1 teaspoon liquid detergent in a gallon jug. Add enough water to make 1 gallon. Put in a few drops of blue food coloring, if desired. Shake and put portion in spray bottle. Spray on a window and wipe dry with wadded-up newspaper.

Linoleum Or Vinyl Cleaner—Use silver polish to clean crayon from linoleum or vinyl floor covering. Silver polish does not dull finish like cleanser.

Carpet Cleaner—Mix 1 tablespoon white vinegar, 1 tablespoon neutral detergent, such as Woolite, and 1 quart water. For spot clean-up, spray on spot and rub with brush or sponge. Dab dry with towel. Also good to use with mechanical rug shampooer.

LAUNDRY

There's no getting around it. The laundry has to be done. These ideas can help you do it quickly and efficiently.

Wrinkle-Free—Take wrinkles out of ribbons by pulling them across clean surface of warm lightbulb or curling iron. Take wrinkles out of clothes left in dryer too long by adding wet bath towel to dryer. Turn on dryer again for 5 to 10 minutes.

Plan Washing—Plan washing schedule so one load of laundry finishes washing as previous load comes out of dryer. Preventing dryer from cooling down between loads saves energy and cuts drying time.

Revitalize Tennis Balls—Pressureless tennis balls can be washed in washer and dried in dryer for 30 minutes to revitalize them for weeks of good play.

Clean Stains From Inside—Stains often come out more easily if you clean them from the inside of garment.

Hairspray Cleaner—Hairspray dissolves ballpoint pen ink from clothing. Spray hairspray on spot and wash as usual.

Easy Zippers—Rub hard-to-pull zippers with pencil lead. They zip with ease.

Shampoo Cleaner—To clean body dirt from shirt collars, rub with an inexpensive shampoo. Shampoo cuts body grease. Pour shampoo into empty, roll-type deodorant bottle for quick use.

A Versatile Hamper—Need a hamper for the kids? Get one that can do double duty. Buy a small plastic garbage can in a bright color with a self-locking lid. Drill holes in the bottom for air circulation. When it's full of dirty clothes, lock the lid and carry the whole thing to the laundry. Wash clothes, wipe out inside of garbage can and put clean, dry clothes back in. Carry hamper back to the kids' room and put clean, folded clothes away.

Trick For Washing Stockings And Pantyhose—While traveling or when you need clean stockings or pantyhose in a hurry, wash them in the sink and rinse thoroughly. Take damp stockings, lay flat in a bath or hand towel and roll up. Squeeze roll between hands as tightly as possible. Unroll, hang over shower bar and stockings will be dry enough to wear in a couple of minutes.

Keep Socks Together In The Wash—When washing for the family, pin pairs of socks together before putting them in the washer. When the wash is finished, pairs are together and you won't have to spend time trying to match them.

IN THE BATHROOM

Most bathrooms are a disaster area when everyone's finished using them. These ideas help you keep your bathroom neat all the time.

Prevent Towels On Floor—Attach heavy-duty snaps to ends of large towels. When fastened to rack, towel becomes a circle. This prevents children from pulling towel to floor while drying hands.

Inexpensive Toothpowder—Use baking soda mixed with salt as toothpowder.

Clean The Toilet Bowl—Put your hand in a plastic bag while you clean toilet. When you're through, remove bag and throw it away.

To clean bowl quickly and inexpensively, pour in 1/2 cup of bleach. Let sit while you clean bathtub, sink and shower. Don't mix toilet bowl cleaners with bleach. It may cause a dangerous chemical reaction. A once-over with a toilet brush will complete cleaning.

Mildew-Free Shower Curtain—If your plastic shower curtain gets mildewed, spray bleach-based tub and tile cleaner on it. The cleaner works quickly to dissolve mildew and you don't have to take your shower curtain down to clean it.

Save Soap Slivers—Save slivers of soap that are too small to use. Store them in a jar with a lid. When you have almost filled the jar, pour in enough water to cover all the soap pieces. Let the soap dissolve, then use the solution to wash your lingerie. Just be sure you don't add soap with cold cream to your jar. It could cause stains.

Keep Glass Shower Doors Clean—Buy a small squeegee cleaner at your hardware store and hang it in your shower. Have family members "squeegee" off the walls when they finish showering. The walls will be dry, so they won't mildew.

Use Towels More Than Once—Some people use towels more than once before washing. If your towel is still damp, put it in the dryer for 5 to 8 minutes on high before bathing, then remove it. When you finish your bath or shower, your towel is *dry* and *warm*.

Make Bathtub Like New Again—Is your bathtub old or banged up? Instead of replacing it, buy a can of epoxy-enamel paint the same color as the tub and paint it. The tub will look like new and you'll save yourself the cost of a new bathtub!

SHOPPING HINTS

SHOPPING LIST

The following ideas will keep you ahead in your shopping plans. A few efficient lists and some handy hints will help you deal with the chore of shopping.

Make up a standard form for shopping week after week. See sample form on this page. No need to draw up a new one each time. Make multiple copies for use throughout the year.

Arrange the list of food items according to the floor plan of your supermarket. Leave a spot to jot down menus. This is valuable for those who plan meals at the grocery store while shopping. Allow a space to write down other errands you can do during your shopping trip.

SHOPPING LIST	
Dairy Products _____	**Menus**
_____	Sunday _____
_____	_____
Meats _____	_____
_____	Monday _____
_____	_____
Fresh Vegetables _____	Tuesday _____
_____	_____
Frozen Foods _____	Wednesday _____
_____	_____
Cleaning Aids _____	Thursday _____
_____	_____
Paper Products _____	Friday _____
_____	_____
Canned Goods _____	Saturday _____
_____	_____
Bakery Goods _____	_____
_____	**Other Errands:** _____
Personal Care Products _____	_____
_____	_____
Miscellaneous _____	_____
_____	_____

TIPS FOR WISE BUYING

FOOD BUYING

Everyone can use a little help at the supermarket. Check out these ideas. They'll help you save money and get through the market in the shortest time possible.

Check High And Low—Grocery stores often display expensive foods at eye level. Check highest and lowest shelves for best-priced canned goods, paper products and other items.

Use A Calculator—Shop with a pocket calculator. Use it to calculate price per pound or ounce and total grocery bill.

Not When You're Hungry—Don't shop for food if you're hungry. You'll buy more.

Buying Meat—When you buy meat, compare price on basis of cost per portion rather than cost per pound. To find that figure, divide total price of meat by number of portions it will provide.

Generally, you can plan on two or three servings per pound of roast beef, pork, lamb, chicken or turkey. Rib chops, spareribs, short ribs, chicken wings or chicken backs yield only one or two servings per pound because they have more bone and fat.

Coupons—Use coupons to help save money on products you normally buy or new ones you want to try. Be sure to compare prices of products using a coupon and similar ones without coupons. You may find product purchased with a coupon is *more* expensive than one without a coupon!

Unit Pricing—Price items by unit to compare prices. To do this, divide total price by number of ounces, pounds or servings in package. It will give you the price per unit. It's easier to compare this price with other unit prices. Some stores now have unit pricing on shelves. Take advantage of it!

Seasonal Specials—Buy seasonal specials. If you want to make strawberry jam in November, buy strawberries in summer when they are cheapest. Freeze and use later.

Bulk Buying—Set aside extra money for bulk buying. During a sale, stock up on nonperishable items you use regularly or perishable items if you can freeze them.

Use Store Ads—Read and compare store ads in newspapers. Even if you prefer shopping at one store, you may find real bargains at another. Use ads to choose special bargains.

Check Prices—When you're choosing several cans of the same product, check individual cans for price differences. Some lots may be priced differently. Search to find the lowest prices.

Use A List—Always make a list before you shop. It'll help you organize your shopping and give you an idea of what you need before you get to the store. Deviate from your list only if you find items on special.

Read Labels And Check Dates—Read labels on packages and check expiration dates. Buy foods that will be usable the longest. You may also need to check labels for nutritional information.

Compare Prices Of Different Forms Of The Same Food—For example, check prices on frozen, fresh and premixed forms of juice. You may find one form cheaper than another.

Buy Dried Milk—Many people don't like to drink dried milk, but why not use it in cooking? Many recipes call for milk and dried milk works well. Mix as much as you need for your recipe. Mix equal portions of dry milk and whole milk for drinking. Most milk drinkers cannot tell the difference.

Take Along A Styrofoam Container—If you have to do errands after food shopping, take along a large Styrofoam picnic container and put cold or frozen items in it to keep cold. Then you won't worry about food spoiling.

Buy Pet Food In Large Quantities—If you have a pet, you know it's expensive to feed it. Buy large quantities of dry food, such as 50 or 100 pounds of dog food. Or buy canned food in cases. Ask your grocer if he'll sell it to you at a reduced price if you buy it in unopened case lots.

SEASONAL SALES

Seasonal buying is always a good idea. No matter what the current market conditions, you can use seasonal sales to keep costs down. The following list suggests items sold seasonally at better prices.

January
Appliances
Electronic equipment, cassette players,
    stereos, radios, TVs
Furniture
Handbags
Housewares
Gift items
Small appliances
Luggage
Men's dress shirts
Sporting goods (fall and winter sports)
Sheets, blankets and other linens
Toys
Women's winter clothing (coats, sportswear)

February
(traditional Presidents' Birthday sales)
Appliances
Carpeting and floor coverings
China, glassware, silver
Gloves and winter scarves
Housewares
Men's clothing (winter)
Sporting goods (basketball)
Winter shoes and boots

March
China, dishes, glassware, silver
Luggage
Ski equipment
Washing machines and dryers

April
(after-Easter sales)
Children's dress clothing
Dresses
Men's suits
Paint and wallpaper
Ranges
Spring coats

May
Carpeting
Mother's Day sales of women's clothing and
gift items
Sheets, blankets, linens
Spring cleaning supplies
Sporting goods (last year's camping and summer
sports equipment)
Tires and auto accessories

June
Father's Day sale of men's clothing and gift items
Furniture
Houses (many sellers want to speed sales at the
end of the school year)
Luggage
Men's clothing
Winter home improvement items (storm doors
and windows)

July
Air conditioners
Bathing suits
Garden supplies
Outdoor furniture
Refrigerators and freezers
Sporting goods (summer sports, baseball
equipment)
Summer clothing, especially sportswear
Summer shoes and sandals
Washing machines and dryers

August
Air conditioners
Automobiles
Back-to-school sales on children's and juniors'
clothing
School supplies
Garden supplies
Linens
Summer sporting goods

September
Car batteries and mufflers
Carpets and floor coverings
Furniture

October
Children's clothing (winter)
China, glassware, silver
Coats
Gloves
Hosiery and lingerie
Winter sportswear
Gardening supplies (flower bulbs and shrubs for
late-fall planting)

November
Children's and juniors' clothing (fall clearance)
Home improvement supplies
Men's dress shirts, suits, outerwear
Women's coats and dresses

December
Automobiles
Children's and juniors' clothing (continued fall
clearance)
Men's suits and outerwear
Sporting goods
Women's coats
Lingerie
Luggage
Women's suits and dresses
Women's party clothes and evening wear
After-Christmas sales of Christmas cards and
decorations

Acknowledgments

THANKS

Today Show: Steve Friedman, Tom Brokaw, Jane Pauley, Bryant Gumbel, Willard Scott

Family: Julian and Norene Thomas, Clyde and Lori Thomas

Photographers: Borge B. Andersen and Associates; Today Show Photos—Raimondo Borea

Artists: Jane Dalley, Greg Thurber

Food Stylists: Mable Hoffman, Janet Pittman

National Companies: Dow Chemical Company, David W. Evans, Inc., Turkey Information Service, Pacific Kitchen, Washington State Apple Commission, Pacific Coast Canned Pear Service, California Table Grape Commission, Florida Lime and Avocado Administrative Committees, Wilderness Foods

Salt Lake City Companies: Mormon Handicraft, The Rose Shop, Bobcos Self-Service Foods, Joe Granato's Fruit and Produce Company

Children in Photos: Braxton Buttorff, Jefferson Buttorff, Kimberly Christensen, Michele Christensen, Thomas Christopher Erkelens, Kourtny Jensen, Ryan Johnson, Bentley Snyder, Hillary Snyder, Taylor Snyder, Tamara Thomas, Christopher Vlam

Special Thanks: Loretta Brown, Mercy Buttorff, Marion Cahoon, Carol Clark, Virginia Conkling, Alice R. Gautsch, Deanna Godfrey, Lynda Hamberlain, Marj Hasler, Steve Hasler, Dona Hathaway, Faye Heimdal, Leora Thurman Hughes, Dianne King, Kathleen Lubeck, David James Nielsen, Donna Nielsen, Bonnie Norder, Ann Rice, Lana Rowland, Janet Schaap, Lynne Snyder, Jackie Stone, Sandi Strange, Margaret Sumsion, Cherie Thomas, Patti Thurber, Doris Turpin, Brian Twede, Madeline Westover, Melvin D. Wilkey, Ranae Williams, Karen Wright

Plus, a hearty thanks to all my friends who have shared ideas throughout the years.

Index